Just Suck It Up

Learn how to stop the excuses and move forward with your mindset, health, finances, and relationships

JOSH SPENCER

Just Suck It Up: Learn How to Stop the Excuses and Move Forward with Your Mindset, Health, Finances, and Relationships

Editing and Interior design by Douglas Williams

Printed in the United States of America.

ISBN: 9781794171251

DEDICATION

For my wife, Melinda. Your incredible love and constant support of me pushing toward my goals and dreams is the only reason why this book was made possible. To my kids, Brody, Alaina, and Madison. You three are the inspiration for this book. I wrote this to teach you that with the right mindset and work ethic, you can achieve the impossible. To my parents, Terry and Teresa. You both have molded me into the man I am today. My integrity, work ethic, and passion for helping others is because of you.

CONTENTS

GET YOUR BONUS MATERIAL

Don't forget to go online and take advantage of all the FREE bonuses mentioned throughout the book.

Visit: www.JoshSpencer.com/book

VIII | JOSH SPENCER

INTRODUCTION

I WOKE UP ONE day and started thinking about my kids and the legacy I wanted to leave behind. Have you ever done that? I hope so. It's important. We aren't just put on this amazing planet to eat, shit, work, and die. That would suck.

Interestingly, many people live this way. They resemble robots, going through the motions without truly living, experiencing the amazing things that life has to offer, or thinking about the legacy they will leave when they're gone. They don't understand that life is limited. It's always the belief, "there is more time," but that time goes by much faster than most people realize. Then it's too late.

Life has a purpose. I'm here for a reason. You're here for a reason. We have to take advantage of our time here by doing the things we want to do, create memories with our loved ones, travel and see the world, be happy and healthy, and most importantly, leave an imprint. We have to leave a legacy. As cliché as it sounds, we each have a responsibility to impact the world in some sort of positive way.

I've been through quite a bit during my short time here on this earth. There are people who've had it much worse, absolutely, but I've dealt with a constant barrage of obstacles over the years. Some of those have been major obstacles, some minor, but each obstacle has served a purpose. I didn't battle everything I did for nothing. You don't go through your struggles for nothing. And yeah, it's very easy to ask, "why me?" when things go wrong. That's human, but we all need to know that it's important to not stop at "why me?" and instead go on to ask, "what lesson can be learned from this or how can me going through this help others?" There is always a purpose for everything. Sometimes we don't quite understand that purpose initially, but eventually it becomes clear.

I'm one tough son of a bitch. I battled what I did because I can handle it. And I've been able to handle and overcome it all. I have my parents to thank for that. When I was just a wee little boy, they taught me our family motto, "Spencers Never Quit." I was never allowed to give up. I just had to push through whatever struggle I was dealing with and figure out how to overcome it. And I did. That motto is one that I have passed on to my kids and they will have a responsibility to pass it on to theirs. It means so much to me that I even got it tattooed on my right forearm. Yes, that's true. I have based my entire life on this motto, and it's a huge reason I've been able to accomplish so much so quickly.

My passion is to give back. It's been that way since I volunteered as a "Big" for the Big Brothers Big Sisters program back in 2000 as a freshman in high school. My struggles and ability to overcome them have provided me with an opportunity to inspire and help others who might be going through the same things or something similar. That is the purpose of my life. That is the purpose of this book. This is my avenue to pay it forward and leave a legacy behind. This is my way to share all the built-up knowledge that's floating around in my head with you and my kids.

When I look at my life, there are four main areas that I feel are my strengths. Ironically enough, they are only my strengths because of my struggles. Strength is built from struggle! But those four strengths are what the book revolves around. The areas are mindset, health, financial, and relationship success. My goal is to provide so much value and pass on enough knowledge to you that you are able to make drastic improvements in each of these areas. I believe you will finish this book with a new understanding that you have the ability and the tools to create an incredible life.

Why the title *Just Suck It Up*? It's how I approach life. When shit happens, I just "suck it up" and deal with it. I don't dwell on the fact that I'm facing another struggle. It's a part of life. We all struggle. I have a choice of either accepting each struggle or bitching and complaining about it. What good does complaining do? Quite frankly, complaining is pointless. It's annoying to the people around you and doesn't help you move forward in any way. When obstacles are thrown my way, I simply accept them, adjust and move forward. I "suck it up" and figure out a solution quickly.

But there is a story behind it as well; quite an interesting one to say the least. When I told my father that I was going to name the book *Just Suck It Up*, he started laughing. He knew exactly what inspired the title. It directly involves him and something that happened to me during a baseball game when I was younger. Let me briefly explain. During a doubleheader when I was about 14, I slid into second base and jammed my thumb pretty damn hard into the second baseman's shoe. I had a feeling I had broken it, especially after I looked down and it was so swollen that it was double its normal size. I walked over to dad, showed him my massive sausage of a thumb, and told him I was pretty sure it was broken. He looked at me with this blank stare and said, "just suck it up and get back out there and play."

So that's what I did. I couldn't grip the bat with my left hand. Instead, I used my palm to help guide the bat to the ball. Basically, I swung one handed. I ended up going 4-for-4 that game with four singles. I was able to overcome my own limitations and beliefs, get out of my own way, make adjustments, push forward, and somehow, some way, find a way to succeed. Eventually when I did go to the hospital, the X-ray showed I broke my thumb in quite a few places. My dad felt absolutely awful, of course, because if he thought it was broken, he would have never told me to "suck it up" and go play.

Even though playing in that game probably didn't necessarily help my thumb, my dad telling me to "just suck it up" taught me some very important life lessons. "Just suck it up" is a phrase that I adopted from that point forward to help me overcome my excuses, take ownership of my failures, and get out of my own way so that I could continuously move forward in life! So, this book is going to teach you exactly how to "just suck it up" and find success in regard to your mindset, health and fitness, finances, and relationships with your spouse, friends, and kids. You're in for one hell of a ride.

Stories teach lessons. Throughout this entire book I'm going to go into quite a bit of detail about my life experiences. It's not that I enjoy talking about myself, but rather, I feel there is a lot to learn from what I've gone through and been able to overcome. What I hope to do by sharing my story is relate to you, give you hope, and inspire you to tackle the obstacles you're facing in your own life. I'm actually going to get extremely vulnerable with you all. This isn't normal for me. Just ask my wife. I'm mostly a non-emotional guy. I can't remember the last time I cried. That's just the way I am. My father raised me to be tough (obviously). And trust me, I understand the importance of occasionally letting out emotions. I just have a very different way of showing how I feel. Crying just isn't one of them. But by me being real and opening up to you, I'm hoping to connect with and inspire you on a whole other level.

THE LOW-DOWN

This book is not for those of you out there who are easily offended. I'm going to be straightforward and honest with you (sometimes brutally honest), just as I would with my fitness and business clients and partners. With the title *Just Suck It Up*, I'm sure you already expected this. As I've already stated, I'm one tough son of a bitch. There are some people who don't like my straightforward, no BS approach. I'm OK with that, only because I am this way to help people move forward. If I was being brutally honest and straightforward just to be an asshole, that's another story; but that's not the case. When I'm straightforward with someone, it's with the right intentions. My goal is to help people change, period. Throughout this book I'm going to tell you what you *need to hear*, not necessarily what you want to hear.

Sugarcoating the truth and validating people's excuses to avoid offending them is not going to help anyone change. That only enables people to think it's fine to continue doing the same things that are leading them down a path of destruction and mediocrity. If I'm not honest with you, aren't I doing you a disservice? Absolutely. Here's the way I see it. If I'm doing something wrong, I don't want someone telling me what I want to hear just so my feelings don't get hurt. Screw that. I want someone telling me exactly what I need to hear so that I can adjust and move forward.

This is how I am going to be with you as you read the book, so just expect it. Sometimes you might get angry but think about what is actually generating that anger. Is it that I'm being an asshole? Or is it that just maybe I'm telling the truth and you feel guilty for the decisions you've made up to this point? Spoiler alert, it's the latter.

I'm probably going to make you feel uncomfortable as you reflect on the decisions you've made up until this very moment in your life. Being uncomfortable is good. That means something is about to shift. That means you are finally taking time to think about where you are in life and where you *want to be*. That's my goal throughout this entire book, to make you feel somewhat uncomfortable. How you ultimately deal with being uncomfortable is totally up to you, but I'm going to teach you how to embrace being uncomfortable, take action, and make permanent changes in your life.

I'm also going to be cursing every now and then. What you will see from me is an absolute transparency. I want to speak to you through writing just as I would talk to my best friends. When I cuss, that's just me being me. I let some words slip out quite a bit. What you read in this book are the exact same things I would tell you in person. I'm not trying to be someone else. I'm a unique character, I'll admit it. I want that uniqueness to show through my writing.

It also isn't for those who don't have a desire to move forward in life. I truly believe that everyone wants to move forward. Nobody has accomplished everything. There's always room to move forward and improve, no matter how young, old, or experienced you are.

Lastly, this book isn't for those of you who are going to read through and proceed to make excuses about why you can't make changes. I can't stand excuses, which you will learn very quickly. However, if you are someone that does make excuses, I'm going to teach you how to overcome them. The goal is to help you get out of your own way.

THE ROADMAP

Do you battle confidence issues? Do you have trouble taking responsibility for your failures? Do you have trouble understanding how to get beyond your failures? Do you battle with an inability to step outside your comfort zone? Are you paralyzed by fear? Do you battle anxiety? Is your mind constantly consumed with negativity? Do you have issues with staying focused and motivated to reach your goals? If so, fantastic. You're just like everyone else. In the first "how-to" section, "Mindset Success," I will address all of these issues and more. I'm going to prepare your mind for success. It would be pointless for me to go into how to improve your health, finances, or relationships if you aren't mentally prepared to do so. It's the first thing I address because without it nothing else follows. I'm going to help you finally get out of your own way and develop a mindset that will lead to success and happiness beyond your wildest imaginations.

The next major section of the book is "Health Success." The truth is that we have a health problem. Many people are overweight or obese. Many people are battling cancer and other diseases. Many people have sleep issues. Many people are too reliant on medication to mask unexplained symptoms. Many people are tired of feeling sick and tired. Sound familiar? Maybe you are dealing with some or all of these issues. Even if you aren't, though, and are extremely "healthy," I'm going to go into great detail about the steps that you can take to become even healthier. I thought I was healthy until I developed a disease. Then I discovered that my idea of "healthy" wasn't all that healthy after all. In this section

I'm going to teach you everything I know about how to become healthy and fit.

Next, I dive into "Financial Success." Are you in debt? Are you living paycheck-to-paycheck? Are you completely unorganized when it comes to your finances? Are you unhappy with your career? Are you looking for other ways to earn additional income? Do you want to have more time? Do you want to build wealth? If so, this section will be perfect for you. The majority of people are struggling greatly with their finances. I'm going to help change that around with some simple steps that anyone can follow.

The last section of the book is "Relationship Success." Answer these questions. Do you and your spouse constantly argue? Has your sex life gone down the toilet bowl? Does your relationship lack communication? Do your kids not listen to you? Do you make promises you can't keep? Do you constantly let down your friends? If so, I'm going to help you make some pretty drastic changes so that you can improve your relationship with your spouse, kids, and friends.

Before I get into any of the "how-to" sections, though, I'm first going to go into some detail about my story. I want you to learn about my family, my work ethic, and my integrity. I need to do so in order to give you a good picture of the type of person I am. I also want you to understand what I went through. I want you to see how I reacted to adversity. That's important. I want you to relate to me. Some of the issues I've dealt with, such as being bullied and living paycheck-to-paycheck, are issues that many people, maybe even you, have dealt with or are currently dealing with. Other issues, such as battling a life-threatening disease, provide important lessons, but aren't quite as common.

Right now, I'm giving you a virtual fist bump. Let's get started.

All About Me

The Early Years

I GREW UP IN a small farm town in Ohio. My sister, Courtney, and I are the only children of my incredible parents, Terry and Teresa, who have been married since 1983. Dad is a hard-headed, stubborn, competitive, and insanely driven individual. He's not really emotional and just tells it like it is. He's a businessman and an ultimate workhorse with an incredible ability to stay calm in tough situations. At the same time, though, he enjoys having fun and spending time with family.

Mom, on the other hand, is one of the most kind-hearted, family-oriented, generous, and calm people I know. She wears her heart on her sleeve. I'm a weird combination of them both. I definitely got my dad's work ethic, ambition, leadership skills, competitiveness, and level-headedness, but my mom's generosity and a family-first attitude. Personally, I think I got lucky because it's a hell of a combination for success and happiness.

I also love to have a good time. I really enjoy traveling, spending time with my wife and kids, and having a few drinks with my buddies while watching sports. I love the outdoors and anything that provides adrenaline. I enjoy snowboarding, dirt bike riding, mountain biking, or anything else that gets the heart racing. Ever since I was young, I have always been extremely active. I hate sitting still and always have to be doing something. My wife makes fun of me about this. It's nearly impossible for me to sit and do nothing for longer than a few minutes. My mind has to be occupied at all times during the day.

Early grade school went smoothly for me, but when I got to about 5th grade, well, not so much. That's when I started getting bullied. I have never been a big kid. Hell, I'm 5'7" now as a full-grown adult and was a peanut back then. And for some reason, I wasn't too confident in myself. I think a lot of that had to do with my over-analytical personality. I constantly questioned whether I was attractive, being judged, liked by others, and good enough.

Bullies were quick to exploit my weaknesses and found joy in picking on me. Part of it's my fault, though, because I always let them. That had to do with a lack of self-confidence. Don't mistake what I'm saying here. I was the victim. What those bullies did to me was wrong. But if I had just stuck up for myself once, there's a great chance they would have left me alone. But I didn't. I mostly sat alone at lunch, played alone at recess, and never really had anyone to sit with in class. I had a few close friends, but that was it. I wanted to fit in so badly, but I never was able to do so.

There was always one group of "popular" guys that especially enjoyed picking on me. There's one particular time that sticks out to me the most. I went to the bathroom and the group of guys followed me in. I went up to the urinal to handle my business and they started talking shit behind me. One of them thought it would be funny to push me into the urinal while I was peeing, causing me to pee all over my sweatshirt. Unfortunately, I wasn't wearing an undershirt, so I had to head back to class with my sweatshirt soaked in piss. When I got back to class, it was obvious they had told everyone, and the entire class stared at me chuckling. It was embarrassing to say the least. Instances like this happened for years.

When I got into high school, though, things started to change. I made the varsity baseball team as a freshman and started doing a little bit of weight training. I also started working with my dad to learn jujitsu so I could defend myself if any of the bullies tried to pick a fight. The more I worked out and the better I got at fighting, the more confidence I gained. Then, one day after school right before baseball practice, the same guys who bullied me for years decided to try to intimidate me again, with one of them getting in my face and putting his finger on my chest. However, instead of backing down like I normally did, I stood up to him, pushed his finger off my chest, looked him dead in the eye and told him to never lay a finger on me again. He didn't know how to respond. He backed down, talked some shit, then walked away. That was the last time any of them picked on me.

Today I'm a huge advocate of anti-bullying. Whenever I hear of anyone getting bullied, it just destroys me inside because I know what they are going through. It's tough. Nobody quite understands just how much it tears you down, beats down your confidence, unless you have been bullied. Whenever I get the opportunity to be able to speak to a kid that is getting bullied, I jump all over it. I want to do everything I can to teach him or her how to stay strong and handle those situations.

As you read through this book, you will see how experiences like this have impacted my life and led me to where I am today. I will come back to this topic later in the book when I address how to handle "haters," since they are basically the same thing as bullies.

MY FAMILY

My beautiful wife, Melinda, and I have three incredible children: Madison, Alaina, and Brody. My family is the most important thing in my life. My wife and I have an incredible relationship and have been married since October of 2011. We've been together, though, since December of 2008. We both are a part of a network marketing business as online fitness coaches. It's what we both do full-time, so we get to stay at home with our kids every day, which is absolutely amazing. I first got involved in the business in 2008 and she joined in 2009. There is no doubt we both love what we do. We each have a passion for helping others and changing lives, which always comes first, but we also love being able to build a business and help others do the same.

What's interesting, though, is how different my wife and I are. It's interesting, I guess, but definitely not surprising. It's almost the exact same situation personality wise with my mom and dad. Just like them, we're basically polar opposites. I already explained my personality type. My wife resembles my mom; very relaxed, patient, kind-hearted, giving, reserved, shy, and just wants to please others. She will do anything to make me and the kids happy. I'm fortunate I found her because, if not, I'd probably be going hard 24/7. She brings a balance to my life that I feel everyone needs, especially those of us who are insanely driven to succeed.

Melinda's especially taught me so much about the balance needed between family and work. At points in 2010 and 2011, I was focusing so hard on building my business and getting our family out of a terrible financial situation that I completely neglected her and my oldest daughter. I've had to put my stubbornness to the side multiple times and make some necessary changes over the years. I did in that specific situation. I believe that's one thing that's unique about me. I'm always willing to change if it's for the better. I'm not the same person today as I was when I met Melinda in 2008 because of the amount of changes I've made. If there are qualities about me that interfere with my relationships or business, I am more than willing to put the work in to change. That's rare. I know it's cliché to say, but Melinda and I truly do complete and complement each other. My kids and her are my everything.

My Fitness & Business Success Story

Baseball became my life from the age of 5 until I graduated college at 22. If you have ever taken a second to think about how the sport works, it's very different than most others. More specifically, it's a failure sport. A "great" hitter in the Major Leagues fails 7 out of 10 times at the plate. The only thing that makes those people "great" is their ability to accept and overcome their failure. Baseball has been one of the main things that prepared me for all the failure I've experienced.

I was fortunate enough to get a scholarship to play baseball in college. When I got there, though, I was still very small — 5'7" and just around 140 lbs. Coach needed me to beef up a little and that's when he put me in the weight room with the other players, got me on creatine and protein, and started me on a strict lifting regimen. By the time my senior season rolled around, I was right around 180 lbs. and insanely strong. I was the guy in the weight room every single morning for at least an hour. Working out was something that I thoroughly enjoyed.

Once I played my last college game, I really felt like a big piece of me was missing and it was tough to deal with the realization that a major chapter of my life was over. I did have plans for after college, though. I majored in business and finance and wanted to become a financial advisor, eventually opening up my own business as a financial planner. I interviewed with quite a few different firms and they all wanted me to come on board. I thought I was on top of the damn world!

Sensing I would succeed with whatever firm I joined, I chose the one offering the highest signing bonus — $3,500. For someone just getting out of college and used to being poor and eating cereal for three meals a day, it felt like a lot of money. I bought myself a suit and pranced around in that thing like I was king shit. Everyone at the office told me I had to "look the part," so that's what I did. Little did I realize that those telling me I had to wear a suit every day were just going along with society's idea of "dressing for success." It wasn't until later that I understood that success comes from your ability to be transparent and "be you." Wearing a suit, that wasn't me. Wearing jeans, a t-shirt and ball cap, that's me.

Anyways, I thought I had everything all figured out, knew exactly what my future would hold. It's funny how the good Lord above stops you in your tracks and has different plans. The more I learned about the financial industry, the more I didn't like it. There are a lot of people in the industry who operate with a lack of integrity. Integrity is one of the most important things in my life.

I was working 14-16 hours every day doing something that I hated doing. When you lack passion for what you do, productivity plummets. I became extremely rebellious and developed a terrible attitude at work. Still, I didn't want to quit. You already know my "Spencers Never Quit" motto and I was determined to live up to it. It became so bad, though, that the only way I could get the courage to call people about insurance was to sit down at the table each night, grab a bottle of rum, and only make the calls when drunk enough.

The stress and long hours at work caused me to stop working out. Combine that with eating at Chinese buffets multiple times a week for lunch and stuffing my face with pizza and fried foods in the evening, and the weight came on quickly. At 5'7" I found myself sitting once again at about 180 lbs., but this wasn't like the same weight I carried in college. I was a fluffy little bastard this time with no muscle mass and with the weight came a lack of self-confidence. Nobody enjoys being overweight and unhealthy. I sure didn't.

Then came the first of two moments that changed the course of my life. Let me pause for a second and explain something very important pertaining to this. When you get to a point in your life when you know you have failed with something and absolutely need to make changes, you have two options. First, you can do what most people do and ignore the need to change just so you don't have to experience the pain associated with realizing you have failed yourself and possibly others. It's easier to stay ignorant and bury the pain, than to let it surface and make a change. The majority of people take this route.

With option two, though, you can let the pain in and use it to motivate yourself to make incredible changes. When you let the pain surface and realize how awful it is to feel that way, you will do whatever is necessary so that you don't have to feel that way again. That is exactly what happened to me. And from this point on, I challenge you to stop playing ignorant and let in the fact that you might have failed yourself or others. Let in the pain! Just like with me, you won't ever want to experience that feeling again and it will motivate you to make changes. Use that as fuel every single day until you change your situation around.

I remember waking up one morning after yet another night of drinking and looking in the mirror just like I did every morning, but this time pausing for a minute. I took a long, hard look at myself and reality hit me like a ton of bricks. I didn't like the person I had become, not just physically, but mentally and professionally as well. As I stood there in my boxers staring at myself in the reflection, I let in the pain that I had failed and was not who I wanted to be. I lacked confidence, was out of shape, drank every night, burned important relationships, and hated my job. It was a low point in my life. Right then and there, though, I made the decision to change and never look back. It all started with me getting myself back into shape. I used the pain as motivation.

I started doing a ton of research to find a complete program that would help me change. I wanted to find one that would force me outside my comfort zone and kick my ass, but also teach me how to eat right. After a few weeks of searching, I couldn't find anything. Then late one night as I sat on the couch flipping through the channels, I came across this infomercial for a home workout program. I got this strange feeling deep inside that I was supposed to continue watching. I did and watched the entire 30-minute segment. What captivated me was that, unlike most workout programs on TV, this one was advertised as incredibly challenging. In a world full of quick, easy fixes, this promised to be different. Right after the infomercial was over, I went online and bought it.

Before I began the program, I swore to myself I would follow it to a "T" for 90 days. That's exactly what I did. It wasn't easy, especially in the beginning. The workouts absolutely kicked my ass and I was the sorest that I had ever been in my entire life. I had trouble brushing my teeth after arm day and sitting on the toilet after leg day. It seriously felt like someone took a baseball bat to my entire body! However, I pushed through it, understanding soreness as a good thing that meant my body was changing.

During those 90 days, I didn't have an ounce of alcohol and never once cheated on my diet. My birthday even fell right smack in the middle of the program, but I never once deviated from the nutrition plan. You see, when I commit to something, I'm all in. That commitment paid off and my reward came as I literally got into the best shape of my life.

Something shifted in me along with my appearance. Already passionate about health and fitness, completing the program just took it to another level. All I wanted to do was help others make the same changes I did. I had found a solution and knew it could help others as well. After I completed the program, I posted my "before" and "after" pictures on a chat forum and spent hours and hours each night answering questions about what exactly I did. I wasn't getting paid for it; I just enjoyed it. It was incredibly fulfilling to be able to inspire and help others make changes just as I did. Plus, it was a nice little escape after working 16 hours at a job that I couldn't stand.

Barbie, my online coach, then asked me to join the business with her, but I told her I just wasn't ready. Plus, I wasn't familiar with network marketing. If you don't know what network marketing is, basically it's a business structure where you are a distributor for a specific company selling products and recruiting others to do it with you. You then help those people build successful businesses of their own. As you sell product, bring people on and teach them how to build a team, there are financial benefits. Each person that joins the network is an actual business owner and has the ability to "pass up" the person that brought them into the business, all depending on their effort. It can be a very lucrative career if built properly.

Anyway, I was still holding onto this flaky dream of miraculously developing a serious passion for financial advising and opening my own business as a financial planner. I'm going to give you some advice. If you have to force something to work, more than likely it's not going to work out. I had fought and forced something to work that I knew deep down inside just wasn't going to work.

After deciding on a whim to take a week-long vacation to escape and think about my future, I knew what I needed to do. I'd be an idiot if I passed up the opportunity to open up my own business as an online fitness coach. July 7th of 2008 was the day I became a fitness coach.

There are two main reasons why I became a fitness coach. First and foremost, I wanted to help people change their lives. This provided me an incredible opportunity to do so. As I've stated, my passion for giving back and helping others goes back to my involvement with the Big Brothers Big Sisters organization. For those of you who don't know, Big Brothers Big Sisters (BBBS) is an incredible organization that helps less fortunate kids. Here's how it works. The guardians of the children enroll them in the program to be mentored by volunteers called "Bigs." Each "Big" is required to spend a certain amount of time with their match each month.

For four years during high school, I was a "Big" to a boy named David. David had a rough life. He and his sister, who is paraplegic, were living with and being taken care of by their grandmother. The father was in and out of the picture and the mother was not around at all. David's grandma enrolled him in the Big Brothers Big Sisters program because she wanted him to have a positive male influence in his life. That's where I came in. I did my best to teach David all the things that my parents taught me when I was young, especially living with integrity and the importance of hard work. Working with David and seeing the impact that I was having on his life was one of the most satisfying things that I've ever experienced.

I always knew that I wanted to have a career where I could give back and help others like that and I thought being a financial planner was the answer. But again, it wasn't what I thought it would be. The more I thought about it, the more I realized that becoming a fitness coach was the answer. Being a coach would allow me to have a career to support my family while helping others in a field I was passionate about — the perfect scenario.

The second reason why I wanted to become a fitness coach was the basically unlimited earning potential. With my financial advising job, I was limited, and I hate being limited. I wanted my income to reflect my effort. That's normally not the case in Corporate America. No matter how hard you work, your boss and upper management control how much you make. That's a fact that most people don't like to admit or even think about. Joining this network marketing team would allow me to build my business and income at my own pace. That's good for people with an insane work ethic like me, but bad for the lazy. Also, I hate working "under" someone. There is nothing worse than working for a boss who feels they are "above you."

A few months after I started my fitness business, I quit my financial advising job and started working for my dad. At the time, he ran a business that did house and business cleanouts. He also ran a document shredding company. He understood my passion for my fitness business and thankfully allowed me to go home early quite often so I could work on it. He's a smart businessman and understood the potential just as I did.

Not too long afterward, in December of 2008, I met Melinda. After dating and eventually moving in together and having a child, we came upon some financial struggles. At the time, I was severely failing with my fitness business because of my immaturity as a business owner. I still was clueless about how exactly to build a successful business and didn't experience growth. I was just 23 years old without any prior business experience, so I faced a lengthy learning curve. I made some money, about a few hundred a month, because I did a great job recommending products, but that's it.

With me working just part-time for my father, we struggled each month to keep up with our bills and rent payments. There wasn't enough income coming in to support our family. We had just enough to get by. We lived in an extremely dangerous, gang-ridden neighborhood for a while, and there was no way I was going to put Melinda and our daughter at risk every day. It was so bad, in fact, that the house across the street blew up because it was a meth lab. Going outdoors during the evening wasn't necessarily the best idea. So, we eventually moved into a tiny one-bedroom apartment in a safer, but more expensive, area. We let our daughter, Madison, have the only bedroom while we slept on a couch. We slept on that couch for three years! To this day, when visiting friends, we tell them that we don't even need a bedroom. Just give us a couch and we are good.

But every month we lived paycheck-to-paycheck. The only thing that kept us afloat was government support, or food stamps. Madison required special formula, which wasn't cheap. Without government support, we wouldn't have been able to purchase $130 worth of formula every few weeks. We definitely had hit rock bottom. We didn't go out to eat, go to the bars, or buy anything that we didn't need. We focused on the necessities and that was it. Having $50-$150 in our account at a time was a normal occurrence. On top of all that, I was about $15,000 in debt with my student loans and needed to pay that back each month. I'm sure many people, possibly even you, can relate.

I mentioned earlier that there were two main moments that shifted the course of my life. The first was that moment in front of the mirror. The second was another moment when the pain hit me hard. We were in the grocery store once again picking up formula and groceries for the week. However, it wasn't Melinda this time who checked out. It was me. Melinda had to run and get something and handed me the food stamps. As I got up to the cashier, who proceeded to ring up all of our groceries, the feeling of failure and guilt overcame me. "What was I doing?" "How could I be OK with this?" I wasn't OK with it. I had failed as a husband. I had failed as a father.

I'm going to be honest with you, there is nothing worse for a man than the feeling of failing your family. Realizing that you are letting down the people you care about most is like someone walking right up to you and taking a sledgehammer to your gut. Most men ignore the fact that they have failed themselves or their family, though. They bury the pain and ignore the truth. They know that, if they let the truth sink in, the pain and guilt will be unbearable. They are right. It is unbearable, but as I already talked about, that feeling leads to change. No father or husband wants to continuously live with the guilt of knowing they have failed their family. Pain leads to action and action leads to change.

It was awful having to hand the cashier the food stamp card to pay for our daughter's formula. It was awful having to worry about whether or not we could afford the $360-a-month rent payment for our apartment. The feeling of failure, the guilt, the embarrassment in that exact moment was overwhelming. For a guy who's supposed to be the provider and supporter of the family, that's a tough thing to swallow. There was a constant knot in my stomach that I couldn't shake. Because I accepted the truth and embraced the emotion, I was ready to change.

For a year and a half, I couldn't make the fitness business work, but I finally understood the opportunity in front of me and resolved to turn it around. Then came a pivotal moment. Not too long after the grocery store incident, I sat my wife down and told her my vision, goals, dreams, and where I believed I could take our family. All I needed was her support while I figured it all out. If I was going to make this work, I knew that I would have to work ridiculous hours. That meant I would have to sacrifice sleep and some family time. As a man who puts family first, that was a tough one for me, but I knew that one year of sacrifice and hard work would lead to a lifetime of freedom.

She understood and offered her full support. From that point on, I spent hundreds of hours researching social media marketing, SEO, and leadership. I read book after book after book. I found myself a few mentors who could teach me how to successfully build a business. I started listening to those who knew more than I. I tried different ideas. Suddenly, it all clicked. That was December of 2009.

A magical year followed in 2010. The business suddenly became clear as I finally got out of my own way. I knew exactly what I needed to do to become successful. All I needed was time. Then came one of the toughest decisions of my entire life. I had to tell my father that I wanted to quit working for him and go full-time with my fitness business. The next day at work with my dad, I remember sitting in the truck and turning to him and saying, "Dad, there's something I need to talk to you about." He looked over at me and said, "Well there's something I want to talk to you about as well." I told him to go first and he said, "I've been thinking, and I want you to take over one of my businesses for me."

Dad owned multiple businesses and felt it was the right time to let me control one of them. Interesting timing, of course. He knew I was destined to be a successful business owner and he was ready to hand over more responsibility. At this point, my stomach dropped to my knees and I said, "Well you're not going to like what I'm about to say, but I want to go full-time with my fitness business."

We just sat in silence for a few minutes. You want to talk about one of the most intense moments of silence I've ever experienced, this tops the list. At first, I thought he was angry, but then he said, "This will be hard on me, but you know I support you with everything that you do and if you feel like this is the direction that you're supposed to go in, I'll support you 100%." He knew my passion for my business and the potential I had as a business owner. As a business owner himself, he respected my decision. That was my last week working for him. The toughest part of it all was knowing that I was putting a lot of pressure back on him, since he was trying to back off from the businesses a bit. In a way, I felt like I let him down, but I knew it was ultimately the right decision. I had to follow my passion and do what I felt was best for my family and for me.

I took a massive risk and went full-time with my fitness business. I'm a firm believer that without risk there is no reward, and this was surely the biggest risk I had ever taken in my life. I turned away a huge opportunity to run one of my father's businesses and work alongside him. Once I made the decision, I never looked back. I worked 14-18 hours a day every day for pretty much that entire year. At the end of 2009, we were still on government support. By the end of 2010, we had established a six-figure income. We got off of government support the moment we were financially capable of doing so and it was one of the greatest feelings in the world. We had done it! We were able to overcome the biggest obstacle in our lives to that point.

As a man who doesn't get emotional, I can't explain to you what it feels like to go from being a failure to providing complete freedom and security for your family. From that point on, my business exploded. From 2010- to 2014, I experienced growth in my business, team, and income that I could never have imagined. We quickly went from a six-figure income to a seven-figure income and I became a millionaire by the age of 27. While most men are still getting out of that "drinking every night stage" at 27, I had been through hell and back and created a million-dollar business.

Today, we are totally debt-free and our businesses continue to thrive. We are now multimillionaires and have the same passion for helping others as we did on Day 1. I wouldn't say I'm special and I'm sure as hell not lucky. I'm a normal guy with an insane work ethic, ambition to succeed, passion for helping others, and a great support system who has the ability to accept failure and make quick adjustments.

WHAT I DO

What do my wife and do as online fitness coaches? We've got a ton of responsibilities. Really, there are three main areas to this business. First, because it's a network marketing business, I lead and mentor the thousands and thousands of people on my team. I spend a lot of time each week mentoring via calls and video conferences, along with developing trainings and running training groups. I'm a busy guy with just this aspect of my business. Another part of the business is the marketing side of it. A lot goes into that. I've hired help, but there are still a lot of things I do on my own, such as all social media marketing and branding. Both Melinda and I are very active on social media and have been consistent with it for years. You can follow both of us on Facebook and Instagram. My IG handle is @TheJoshSpencer and hers is @CoachMelinda8. My Facebook page is Facebook.com/TheJoshSpencer and hers is Facebook.com/MelindaFitness.

The last part of my business has to do with helping others achieve their fitness goals. It's hard to say which part of the business I like best because they are all enjoyable and fulfilling in their own way. But I can tell you that this aspect is the most fulfilling. I've had the privilege of watching and helping people make some drastic transformations over the years. There's one transformation in particular that I always think about.

Braden came to me early on in my coaching career asking for guidance. What's interesting is that he found me through my transformation video on YouTube. He told me it inspired him to make a change and he started going to the gym and eating right. When he reached out to me for the first time, he had already lost something like 40 lbs., down from around 290 lbs. When I first started helping him, it was mostly on the supplement and nutrition aspect. He was going to the gym and getting results so there was no reason to push him to do something else. However, he wanted to do the home workout program that I did, but it was just a little too extreme at the time because he was still pretty overweight.

At the time, I had never worked with someone that overweight, but was willing to do whatever I could to help him make the change. The process was the same with the exception of some heavy modifications in the beginning stages. And I have discovered that most people who are very obese suffer from some bad addictions. Not necessarily drug addictions, but food addictions. When emotions get the best of them, they find their escape in food, especially sugar. As you will discover shortly, excess sugar intake is a big reason for the obesity epidemic.

Braden knew he had a food issue and was willing to make whatever changes he had to in order to get results. He was the quickest person I ever worked with to fight through the addiction and commit fully to what I recommended. However, I noticed something in the middle of his journey. He had shaken the food addiction but traded it for a workout addiction. Instead of using food to cope, he worked out obsessively. He lost a lot of weight, which he needed to do, but he took it just a little too far and became extremely skinny. I believe he even mentioned he might have battled anorexia at one point. But he caught on to what was happening and changed course. At 6'5" he got down to 168 lbs., but then got back up to right around 180-190 lbs., which is where he needed to be. He looked healthy and strong at that weight.

Braden eventually signed up on my business team and we ran into and officially met each other for the first time on a rewards cruise. What he said to me is engraved in my mind to this day. He said to me, "I don't know if you know this, but before we connected, I was considering taking my life. Josh, you literally saved my life." I'd be lying if I told you that I didn't begin to tear up. Those are powerful words that keep me focused on doing what I do every single day. On that trip, Braden and I became friends and we have remained friends to this day. In fact, we've been on multiple ski trips together and he's even come and stayed with us quite a few times. Here is a message he sent to me not too long after that cruise:

"I just wanted to let you know how unbelievably thankful I am to have you in my life. You are literally the closest thing I've ever had to a big brother, and you are my #1 role model. In addition to the thousands of other people you've helped, take a few extra seconds today and remember that because of you, I'm here today. You literally saved my life man, and I can't describe how thankful I am to you."

Sometimes the person they become is not even remotely close to the person they were before, in a good way of course. It's an incredible thing to witness and be a part of. It's a big reason I wake up every morning with a smile on my face and why I keep pushing so hard with my business every day. It's the reason why I became a coach in the first place.

My Integrity

Spencers operate with integrity. Part of the reason for all my success is that I have always operated with integrity. Integrity is one thing I will absolutely never sacrifice for anything. Success means nothing if you lose who you are along the process.

A great leader lives their life, both in the public eye and in private, with the utmost integrity. I have both my parents and grandparents to thank for teaching me the importance of living life with integrity at a young age. Not only did they constantly talk to me about it, they were positive examples of it by the way they operated their own businesses and always put family first.

I had the privilege of growing up and watching my grandpa create this family-type culture within his grocery business that you just don't see much of anymore. My dad currently owns three businesses (possibly more by the time you read this) and operates the same way. In addition, integrity in my family goes well beyond just the business world. My grandpa and grandma married when they were young and stayed together until the day my grandpa passed away. He was a loyal man who always put family first. I remember so many times growing up spending time with him when he could have been doing something business-related. However, he knew that family is the most important part of life and always made time for us. I miss him every day. He had such an impact on my life that it's hard to describe to you in words. He was the absolute perfect example of a man of integrity. I strive to be more like him every single day. Just like with my grandparents, my parents have stayed married as well and both have been very faithful to one another. Melinda and I are the same way. I'm not saying that divorce is terrible because sometimes it's necessary. But many times, divorce happens because one or both people in the marriage acts with a lack of integrity.

I focus my efforts every day to be the positive example to my kids that my parents and grandparents were to me. It's a legacy I hope to pass down for all future Spencer generations. Every day I'm forced to make decisions and each time I do, I ask myself if the choice I make will line up with who I am and if it will be a proper example for my kids. If it does address both situations, then I move forward. If it doesn't, then I don't. It's simple. When it comes to my individual integrity, there is never a gray area. It either lines up with my values or it doesn't.

MY WORK ETHIC

Another reason why I've been so successful with fitness, business, and my relationships is because of my work ethic. The truth is that it's unmatched. It's not arrogance, it's confidence. Let me share a story.

I mentioned already that when I was 12 years old I started playing travel baseball. I had to try out to make that team. This team was one of the best in the state and contained very high-level players. I, on the other hand, was not a high-level player. I would even go as far as saying that I was probably the worst player on the team. No, I take that back, I was the worst player on the team. There's no shame in admitting it. I was an average ballplayer at best. Good enough to make the team, yes, but still very average. How I even made the team is a mystery, but nonetheless, I made it happen. Maybe dad paid them? Just kidding, I hope.

They put me in the nine hole and threw me out in right field, both spots normally reserved for the worst person on the team. If you would ask my father today if I was a great player back then, he would shake his head that I wasn't. He knew I needed help to improve my game. It was at that point that he decided to get me batting lessons. He knew that the only way I was going to be able to get better was to be taught by a professional. Dad could have taught me himself, but he would have been only able to help me so much. He also understood that taking batting lessons is one thing but practicing consistently what is learned during the lessons is where the true magic happens. How many times do people learn something, then never apply it? It's common. In fact, the majority of people are this way. Why? Because it takes effort and it's normally well outside their comfort zone.

Look at it this way: There are a ton of books on how to create a successful real-estate business. If everyone read those books and applied what they learned, they would be wildly successful. However, only a select few will actually take the time to read the book, and then an even smaller number of people would act on what they learned. And yes, that will even be the case with my book. It's loaded with information, but the truth is that the majority of you won't do anything with it! I truly hope, though, that you actually do take action. But there's a reason only a small percentage of people ever become successful. They just lack the work ethic.

I wasn't someone with a great work ethic initially, though. I had to learn it. At 12 years old, I remember playing video games one night and hearing my dad yell up to me from downstairs. He said, "Hey Spence!" "Yeah dad?" "Hey, come downstairs in the basement." "Um O-OK dad." I reluctantly went downstairs and when I got to the bottom of the stairs, I saw my dad standing there with a net and tee set up, along with a bucket of balls and my bat. He said, "Grab your batting gloves, you're going to hit 500 balls off the tee." I have always respected my dad, so I listened to him and hit 500 balls off the tee, practicing what I learned from my batting lessons. However, it wasn't without a little bitching and moaning. Afterwards I was tired, my hands were blistered and bloody, and I was irritated that I had to take time away from playing Donkey Kong to hit so many damn balls off the tee. Next night, same thing. The following night, same thing. This went on every night for a few months. Each night he videotaped me hitting so that I could take a few swings and watch the recording to analyze whether or not I was doing something wrong. When we watched the recording and did find that I was making a mistake in my form, we quickly made adjustments and continued the process until my swing looked fluid and strong. We also moved the tee all around, forcing me to pull the ball, hit it up the middle, and take it opposite field.

After a few months of this process, I started noticing something change. During the games, I could see the ball better and was making better contact and getting more hits. Instead of pulling every ball, I began to hit it where it was pitched. At that point, I realized that dad was trying to teach me an important lesson. He was trying to show me that, if I wanted to get better, I had to work harder. The only way to become great at something is to work hard with it every single day. Through time and commitment, I knew I could become one hell of a ballplayer. And I did. I ended up getting a scholarship and played ball for four years in college.

My work ethic has helped me succeed in many areas of my life. When I want to accomplish something, I work hard with it every day to make it happen. With the right work ethic and consistency, you can too.

THE GREATEST CHALLENGE OF MY LIFE

It's interesting how the good Lord above doesn't put things in front of you that you can't handle. Once again, there is a purpose to everything, which I now realize was true when I was presented with yet another obstacle, this time much greater than those that came before it. I had developed a chronic disease.

When a fitness coach develops a chronic disease, there is some irony behind it. How does a guy who works out and takes care of himself every day contract a disease? I asked myself that over and over again. It didn't make sense to me. Now it does, of course, but I will get to that later.

But in 2015, I started developing some very strange symptoms. First, I started having pain in the back of my head on both sides where the neck meets the skull. Second, I developed awful fatigue, so bad that I felt like sleeping all day every day. Next came stomach issues, nausea, and night sweats. It was common for me to wake up completely soaked in the middle of the night for no apparent reason. A week or two later, I began experiencing terrible dizziness and breathing issues. There were many times when dizziness left me unable to stand up. I even landed in the E.R. because of the breathing issues. The last of the symptoms to appear were pretty scary. I started having neurological problems, such as slurred speech, memory loss, brain fog, and anxiety and panic attacks. I was deteriorating at a very fast pace.

When the first of the symptoms began, I went to my family doctor to try to figure out what was going on. He seemed just as confused as me and ran multiple blood tests to search for something major happening inside my body. All of the tests came back relatively normal. He then was convinced that it was all in my head and tried to prescribe painkillers and anxiety medication. He wasn't interested in digging to figure out the root cause of all my symptoms. He would rather mask my symptoms and send me on my way. Unfortunately, this is the way that many doctors operate.

Eight doctors later, I got fed up and decided to take matters into my own hands. If they weren't going to figure this out, I sure as hell was. As the months went by, I progressively got worse to the point where I couldn't function normally. I then began to treat this illness like I do my business and decided to do heavy research to find a solution. I knew that it was up to me to figure it out and I was determined to do just that.

In my research, I discovered two possible culprits that could be wreaking havoc on my body and not show up on any testing: intestinal parasites or Lyme disease. I initially got treated for parasites, but quickly realized that wasn't the problem. I then decided to seek help from a Lyme specialist and within the first few minutes of talking with him and explaining my symptoms, he diagnosed me with Lyme. However, that wasn't good enough for me. I wanted additional testing to verify. We then took a special test from a company called iGenex Labs and it came back positive for a few bands of Lyme Disease.

Then I found out Melinda was pregnant with our son. It hit me like a ton of bricks and quite frankly, scared the shit out of me. All I kept thinking about was being dead (because I truly felt like that's where I was heading) and never knowing my son, or still being extremely sick when he arrived. I kept thinking about all the things I wanted to do with him, like riding a dirt bike, snowboarding, playing catch with him, and teaching him the sport of baseball. There was no way it would have been possible given where I was at the time with my health. Hell, I couldn't even work or work out because I was so sick! How was I going to be the father that I wanted to be? But knowing he was arriving in nine months became my biggest motivator to figure out a solution and heal quickly.

If it wasn't for dealing with Lyme Disease and knowing my son was arriving, I would have never made the shift to a true healthy lifestyle. I thought I was healthy before, but my idea of "healthy" then is not even close to what it is today. I had gained some basic knowledge of health and nutrition when I became a fitness coach, but it's nothing compared with the amount of knowledge I have now after battling and conquering a chronic disease.

After I was officially diagnosed with Lyme and learned about Brody arriving, I began doing an incredible amount of research into naturally healing from disease. I watched countless videos, read countless studies and articles, and read multiple books trying to learn everything I possibly could about living with Lyme so that I could live a normal life once again.

I learned about the various toxins in the food we eat, water we drink, supplements we take, and the products we put in our bodies daily and how they beat down the immune system. I learned the importance of detoxing on a regular basis and how to do so. I learned the role that healthy fat plays in reducing inflammation and improving immune system function. I learned how to heal and restore gut health. I learned how various herbs and essential oils can be powerful healing agents. I fully began to understand the role that sugar intake plays in the development of disease and cancer. And I learned about the importance of vitamins and their roles in the body.

Lyme Disease isn't conquered easily. All you have to do is go to any Lyme forum on social media to quickly discover just how much that statement rings true. I joined quite a few and there were thousands of posts from people who have suffered for years without making any progress. In all honesty, it was depressing to see all the people depressed and suffering. Chronic Lyme is a nasty disease, but no matter how much negativity and lack of hope I found in the forums, I stayed positive and believed that I could get myself healed up enough to be where I wanted to be when my son was born.

I started on an antibiotic plan per doctors' recommendations, but eventually stopped because I understood through research that I would never truly heal unless my body became strong enough to fight this disease on its own. I made some progress with antibiotics, but the real progress came after I stopped and went completely natural with my healing treatment. After applying everything I learned about healing from disease and committing entirely, I slowly began to get better and my symptoms began to disappear. As each month passed, I made more and more prog-ress and eventually was able to get back to a normal life.

My energy returned, I could work out again, snowboard and ride a dirt bike like I used to, play with my kids again, and get back to having an incredible relationship with my friends and family. And by the time Brody arrived, I was about 85% better! Today I am symptom free. The only reason I was able to overcome this disease is because I never stopped learning and believing in myself, had an incredible support system, was 100% committed to healing, and put in the work.

So why did I go through all that? Because God knew I was strong enough to handle it. He knew I would figure out a solution. He knew that the knowledge I would gain from this experience could help thousands and thousands of people. Not only am I now able to better help my fitness clients, but I am able to give hope to the hundreds of thousands who are dealing with this debilitating disease that is destroying so many lives.

Now you have an idea of the type of person I am and the type of obstacles that I've been forced to overcome. It's time to move on to the "how to" sections of the book. I'm excited for you because the rest of the book is going to give you the knowledge and motivation needed to make some incredible changes in your life. Here we go.

Changing Your Mindset

It's time to focus a lot of attention on what I believe is the most important part of the book, "Changing Your Mindset."

Many people struggle with proper mindset. In all actuality, it's normal. Too many people think they are alone then they are dealing with mindset issues, such as low self-confidence, anxiety, depression, excuses, negativity, and fear, but they are not. I've dealt with all of these issues at one point or another. Millions of others have as well and still do. You are not alone! So yes, take a deep breath, relax, you are not some freak. You are human. There's a good chance that every single person you walk by at the grocery store is battling something internally. The great thing, though, is that you can change it with the proper work ethic. I'm going to help you do so.

The goal in this section is to help you develop a mindset that will prepare and lead you to success. The truth is that success with anything, whether it's your relationships, finances, or health, doesn't follow without proper mindset. They go hand in hand. Develop a proper mindset and everything else will follow.

Many of my clients attempt to make health changes when they aren't mentally prepared to do so. It never works. They can try as hard as they can to make changes, possibly even making it months into their journey and seeing some results. But improper mindset will always come back to haunt them. It's unfortunate, but I've seen it happen many times. I've even seen people lose hundreds of pounds only to put the weight back on a year later. How does that happen? They don't focus as much time on changing their mindset and addressing certain personal issues as they do their body. It has to be synergistic. They have to work just as hard on improving mental strength as they do their workouts and nutrition. You can't change your life if your mind isn't in the right place.

Someone who loses a significant amount of weight may look better, but make no mistake, they are still battling the demons that led them to that dark place they found themselves in before they started making changes. The demons may be rooted in issues from their past, excuses, low self-confidence, anxiety, negative thoughts, fear, or drug and food addictions. Maybe something else entirely. The thing is, all of these issues don't just go away overnight. It takes an incredible amount of change, patience, time, and effort to overcome them.

Deep-seeded issues, maybe ones dating to childhood, don't suddenly disappear after reading one positive-thinking book. Sometimes it takes years of effort to reverse the damage done. For example, maybe you deal with low self-confidence. Whenever you want to do something, you tell yourself you're not good enough, so you just never do it. If you've been that way since you were a kid, it's going to take a lot of effort and time to get you to believe in yourself again.

It's hard for most people to handle those issues on their own. Some can, but most can't. I'm one of those people who can, but I'm extremely rare when it comes to this. Even I have to research like crazy to learn how to handle certain issues I encounter. Most people need someone to teach them exactly how to overcome these issues and to make sure they are staying positive and on track when those demons reappear, which will be quite often. They need that accountability and guidance, maybe from a coach like me, a family member, friend, or sometimes even a psychiatrist or therapist. With help, they can learn how to shift their mindset and properly handle setbacks.

It's so important for them to realize, too, that setbacks are common. They are going to happen. Never in my life have I met someone who hasn't dealt with multiple setbacks on their way to success. We all experience setbacks in our marriage, relationships with our friends and kids, business, and yes, even in our health journey. I'm a decade into my health and fitness journey and the number of setbacks I've experienced is off the charts! Injuries, plateaus, sicknesses have all set me back at some point. But I continue to have success because I understand how to overcome adversity. I'm going to teach you how to do so as well.

Let me share a story. While being bullied from 11 to 15 years old, I dealt with some pretty serious confidence issues and struggled to properly handle failure. Those two issues alone really hurt how well I played baseball. I had the work ethic, so why was it that I was still an average player? I had the proper mechanics after practicing at home every night, but I lacked the proper mindset. It's no different than the people I mentioned above. They had all the tools to make incredible, lasting changes, but their mindset held them back from achieving their full potential.

That was me with baseball. I constantly told myself I wasn't good enough. I got extremely down on myself when I failed. Negative thoughts consumed my mind. "What if I strike out again?" "What if the ball is hit to me and I drop it?" "What if dad gets upset that I'm not playing well?" "What if I do bad enough my coach will bench me?" All of these thoughts went through my head during every game. I don't care how much talent you have, nobody can be a great ballplayer with that attitude. You think Babe Ruth went up to the plate with that attitude? No way. He pointed to where he planned to hit the ball with swagger.

Then came the day that shifted my life forever. I was 15 years old playing a doubleheader in my summer league. For some reason, that day I was having a real tough time seeing the ball at the plate. The first at bat, I struck out. Like normal, I couldn't stop thinking about what I was doing wrong and why I wasn't seeing the ball well. I put my head down, walked back to the bench, and just couldn't shake the fact that I struck out. When I was out in the field, I wasn't focused on what was going on in the game. Rather, I was still thinking about the strike out.

When I got up to the plate for the next at bat, all I could think about was not striking out again. Instead of picturing myself hitting the ball right back up the middle for a base hit, I saw myself whiffing for the third strike. My fear and negativity got the best of me and I struck out once again. I walked back to the bench, launched my helmet at the fence, dropped a few "F bombs" and, just like the previous time, I couldn't stop thinking about it. I struck out two or three more times during that doubleheader and got so worked up and pissed off at myself that my coach benched me. He knew that, given the state I was in, I wouldn't be able to help the team.

That was the first time that I'd ever been benched, and it was a huge blow to my already low self-confidence. I went home that evening devastated and even contemplated quitting the summer league and baseball for good. That would have never happened, of course, because of our "Spencers never quit" motto, but it doesn't mean I didn't think about it. I'm pretty sure Dad would have killed me anyway because of all the money spent on lessons and to play for one of the top teams in the country. But I wasn't enjoying playing the game anymore because I overanalyzed every failure and let it affect me negatively.

Once I got home, I ran up to my room, shut my door and sat at the foot of my bed on the floor with my head in my hands. All the negative things in my life got to me and I broke down. Suddenly, my Dad walked in and tossed a book on my bed. He looked at me, said "read this book," and walked out. That's it. I respect my dad, so when he tells me to do something, I don't bitch and complain, I just do it. I picked up the book and it was *The Magic of Thinking Big* by David Schwartz.

So yes, at 15, I was introduced to personal development. I started reading the book as soon as dad left the room and within the first few pages it was obvious the book was going to change my life. That it did. I read it over and over again, took as many notes as possible, highlighted and marked certain important sections, and applied everything I learned to my life on a daily basis.

Make note something I said there. I said I "applied everything I learned to my life on a daily basis." You're going to see me drill this hard throughout this book. Success never occurs without action. It's like someone giving you the master key to a room that contains $10M, but you never actually use the key to unlock the door. Instead you just stand there with the key in hand staring at the lock. Too many people spend too much time learning and not enough time applying. That's pointless.

Through that book, I learned certain exercises that taught me how to replace my negative thoughts with positive ones. For someone who was bullied daily and mentally beaten down, this was no easy task. Negative thoughts filled my mind and it took time and effort to replace those negative thoughts with positive ones. It worked. Suddenly, I walked around the school with a new swagger. I no longer looked down when I walked the halls. I looked up, stood tall, and looked people in the eye. I became a completely different kid and ball player!

The Magic of Thinking Big also taught me how to overcome fear. I had to go through a self-realization stage and understand just how much I allowed fear to control my life. Fear held me back from success. Once you think about it, fear controls most people's lives. Hell, even well into adulthood, many people remain controlled by fear! It's a big reason the majority of people can never achieve any type of happiness or success. They constantly live in fear. But once I stopped letting fear control who I was, only then could I make drastic strides forward in all aspects of my life, from my relationships to my baseball career.

The same goes with understanding how to handle failure. Like it or not, failure is going to happen. Whoever said that failure is not an option surely knows nothing about success. Avoiding failure leads to a less than average life. Once I stopped worrying about failing and embraced that it was a part of the success process, everything in my life improved. Once you get to the point where you embrace failing, a weight lifts off your shoulders.

As you can see, years of personal development and effort have led me to a much different place mentally than where I was when I was younger. It was a process, a very difficult one. What I'm going to do is teach you everything I've learned about having an excellent mindset and the process for developing one. Understand, though, that this process is going to be challenging, especially if your mind has been in a bad place for years. Don't expect to make changes overnight. Don't get frustrated. Take a deep breath, follow my advice, practice proper mindset daily, and stay consistent with it. Through time and effort, you will develop a success mindset.

Now I'm going to address 10 areas that I feel are important for proper mindset. Here's my list:

1. Overcoming excuses.
2. Eliminating negative, self-demeaning thoughts.
3. Handling failure.
4. Conquering fear.
5. Understanding the toxicity of instant gratification.
6. Overcoming laziness.
7. Finding Your Focus and Staying Motivated
8. Setting Goals
9. Eliminating procrastination and taking action.
10. Gaining self-confidence and belief.

Pay close attention to the coming section and highlight. Yes, bring out your highlighter and write all over this damn book. You won't hurt my feelings. Nothing would please me more than seeing you post a picture on my Facebook page of your book highlighted in multiple different colors! I encourage you to do so. Your mindset plays *THE* biggest role in your success, and not just with your health. With all aspects of life!

STEP 1: OVERCOMING YOUR EXCUSES

Do you constantly come up with reasons to justify your failures? You might not think you do, but you probably do. Most of the time, you probably don't even realize you're making them. That stems from years and years of lying to yourself so much that those lies eventually become truths. It gets to the point where you actually believe your own excuses! Just because you believe your excuses are valid, though, doesn't mean they actually are. They aren't. That's the truth. This is a major area of mindset that you need to immediately work on changing. Excuses are simply holding you back.

What exactly are excuses? I probably could look it up in the dictionary, but I wanted to create my own definition. I would define excuses as illegitimate reasons people create for why they can't do something or failed with something just to make themselves feel better for giving up or never taking action in the first place. How's that for a hard dose of reality? I'm hoping at this point you're beginning to think about certain instances where you have used or currently use excuses, such as with your job, marriage, or finances. The first step is acknowledging there is an issue. Damn, I sound like a therapist here, but if you are making excuses and continue to ignore the fact that it's happening, you're not going to be able to make the necessary changes to move forward.

I don't make excuses anymore, but this wasn't always the case. At 15, I realized that excuses ruled my life. If I lost in a video game to a buddy, it was because he cheated, never because he was just flat out better than me. If I got winded and couldn't keep up with everyone during conditioning after practice, it was because of my asthma, never because I was out of shape. I could go on and on with specific examples.

Once I made the mindset shift at 15, though, I literally eliminated all excuses from my life. I now take responsibility for everything, both good and bad. When I fail at something, I ask myself what I did wrong, rather than blame it on someone or something else. This is exactly the process that I want you to start using. Taking full responsibility for anything that happens in your life is the only way to move forward. People really do buy into their own bullshit excuses and it's causing them to remain stagnant in their lives and never experience any type of success.

Next, I'm going to go into some very specific examples of areas where I see most people making excuses. Please go into this with an open mind. How I address some of these might make you angry, but what I explain is the truth. Get beyond your anger, think about whether or not you use each excuse, and if so, how you can stop making that excuse.

'I don't have the time'

As a fitness coach, I hear excuses constantly, the most frequent one being "I don't have the time." I'm about to destroy that excuse very quickly. If you want something badly enough, you find the time. Permanently implant that phrase in your brain. Whenever you find yourself saying "I don't have time," what you really mean is "this is not a priority." This goes with all excuses. If it was a priority you would find the time.

Whenever people use the "I don't have time to work out" excuse with me, for example, I like to use very specific examples to prove them wrong. My favorite one has to do with my father. I explain how he owns three businesses, but still gets up at 4 a.m. every morning to fit in an hour-long workout. He does so because it's a priority for him, no matter how busy his day will be. He could easily make an excuse, but he doesn't.

People use the "I don't have time" excuse for everything. They use it to explain why they can't make changes to their health. They use it as to explain why they can't build a side business. They use it to explain why their marriage is failing. They use it to explain why they can't hang out with their best friend who has been there for them since second grade. They use it to explain why they can't spend time with their kids. The "I don't have time" excuse lets people continue on a path of unhappiness and mediocrity.

We are all busy, some busier than others. But that doesn't mean that we can't be creative and make the time. Again, if it's a priority then you will get creative to find the time. Maybe that means not watching your favorite TV show each night. Maybe that means doing a home workout program instead of spending time driving to a gym every day. Maybe that means not going out with your buddies for beer and wings during the football game and taking your wife out on a date instead. Maybe that means not going out with your coworkers for lunch every day so that you can spend that hour working on your side business. Maybe that means not picking up your phone and browsing the Facebook News feed when you have downtime at work. There is always time. You just have to find it.

Something you can do is write down your list of priorities each day. When you create that list, rank them accordingly and move on to the next only after you complete the previous. Doing this will assure that you do the things you *need to do* each day and only do the things you *want to do* after the main priorities are completed.

Maybe as you read this you're thinking that you still don't have the time. If so, I want you to pause for a minute or two and really think about what you're doing. No really, actually think about what you're saying. You're just holding yourself back. That's it.

Who are you trying to convince? Nobody else cares if you "don't have the time." I don't care, your mom doesn't care, uncle Billy doesn't care. Your excuses affect nobody but you. You either choose to find the time and make a change or you don't.

excuses affect just you

I can assure you, though, that the latter leads to a place you're not going to want to go. Disease, cancer, and obesity all loom down that path. Financial disaster, a failed marriage, and a terrible relationship with your kids also linger down that path. You can ignore it all if you want, but trust me when I say that it will hit you smack in the face harder than a Bruce Lee punch! Then you're going to reflect on your past and say, "Well shit, if only I would have found the time." Don't ever allow yourself to have to go through that.

Don't confuse an excuse with a legitimate reason. Sometimes there are legitimate reasons why people don't have the time. I get that. However, 99% of the time it is within your control. You have to be able to properly differentiate between the two. If it's not in your control, then it's not an excuse. If it is in your control, then it's an excuse. It's not complicated. But if you want to move forward with something that is important to you, you're just going to have to find a way to find the time.

'I don't have the money'

The other excuse I hear often is "I don't have the money." This always makes me laugh because most of the people who use this excuse with me are clueless about what my wife and I went through financially. You already know that story. What I didn't explain, though, was how I found ways to invest in my business and health even when I thought I couldn't afford it.

In 2009 especially, I had to get very creative. I knew that if I wanted my business to grow I had to invest in personal development books and travel to various events around the country to learn from others who had built successful businesses. If that meant I had to sell stuff online to afford those things, that's what I did. If that meant we had to purchase all of our food in bulk, that's what we did. If that meant I had to work out an agreement that allowed me to have a couch to sleep on at a specific event, that's what I did. There were also certain supplements and programs I found ways to purchase because I understood the importance of doing so for my business and health. I can't recommend something I don't use. If I do, I become a slimy salesman. I had to test out certain supplements, nutrition plans, and programs to see if they would work for others. Somehow, someway we were able to make it all happen with very little money in our bank accounts. Getting beyond the "I don't have the money" excuse is a big reason I was able to get our family out of that situation.

Invest in your self

The longer you keep putting off investing in yourself, the longer you're going to remain in the same situation. I don't understand when people tell me they can't afford to make positive changes in their health by purchasing better quality food or a workout program proven to work. I'm not talking about purchasing a video game, I'm talking about investing in something to actually improve your quality of life!

Excuses become so deeply rooted in our way of thinking that it's become a way of life. People keep trying to convince themselves that somehow, some way their situation is different when it's not, not at the core. Doing this makes them feel better about their shitty situation. Or maybe they are just really looking for a pity party, who knows. But the reality is that these are the type of people who will always be stuck in their current situation. They can't get out of their own way. Their mindset causes them to be ignorant of the fact that there are always different ways to make a change. There are always options! But not if you don't accept responsibility and fully understand that you are in control. That is the first step. When you accept responsibility and get out of your own way, then different options will present themselves.

Here's one way that anyone can make money. Garage sales are fantastic because you can get incredible quality used items cheaper than you can find them anywhere else. People hold garage sales because they want to quickly get rid of items, not get rich. The deals that you can find are ridiculous. If you spent an entire day going to garage sales and bought $50 of good quality items, I can almost guarantee you that you could turn around and sell those items on eBay for five to six times the amount, just as long as you do a little research. Again, smartphones make doing research easy today. You can do research on the spot. If you see something you think you would be able to turn around and make a quick profit on, bring up eBay or Craig's List on your phone and find the going price. Just a little time and effort and you could easily make $400-$600 or more during one weekend! You can use the exact same process with the Facebook Marketplace. But all this takes time and effort. Lazy people won't want to put forth that type of effort and would rather live their lives complaining about how life sucks and keep making excuses when opportunities to change do arise.

When people I'm trying to help tell me that they can't afford to change their health right now, I always ask, "Can you afford not to?" Nobody can afford not to. Have you seen the cost of cancer treatment? Go ahead, look it up on Google real quick. We're talking tens or hundreds of thousands of dollars! What about the cost of dealing with a chronic disease? It's much more than the amount that you would spend on investing in a set of weights, workout program, and nutrition plan. In just two years, I spent well over $10,000 out of my own pocket paying for Lyme treatment.

Put cost to the side. I haven't even talked about the effects that poor health decisions now will have on your amount of active years. Like it or not, if you don't take action now with your health, the amount of active and healthy years you will have significantly decreases. As someone who is very active and has children, I want to be able to snowboard or dirt bike with my kids well into my 60s and possibly 70s. If I remained on the path I was on in early 2008, that would have never happened. Rather, I would be that 60-year-old with a cane, overweight, and taking 30 different medications a day complaining about my aching back.

I want you to think about one other aspect in all of this. Let's say that it does cost you $200 a month (that's a stretch) to shift from a poor diet to an all-organic diet and invest in a complete workout program or personal trainer. Let's say you also have children, which many of you probably do. I will get into this later in the book, but as a parent you set the example for your children. Your kids do what you tell them to do and, more importantly, show them what to do. You are a leader by example. That $200 you just spent on improving your health not only changed your lifestyle, but changed your family's as well. You can't even put a price tag on that!

If you still tell me you can't afford it, you need to take a step back and do some self-reflecting. Again, you're just holding yourself back. People need to start focusing on the bigger picture. They need to understand how the decisions they make now will affect their future! "I don't have the money" is just as bad as the "I don't have time" excuse. Later in the book, in the "Financial Success" section, I will teach you different ways that you can find more money to invest in yourself.

'I'm too old'

For every excuse that someone tells me, I will always have a story to disqualify it. "I'm too old" is just another one of those excuses. For this story, I'm going to talk about my parents. When I first started making changes to my health back in 2008, they wanted nothing to do with it. However, my dad's weight began to spiral out of control and he started developing some health issues (I'm pretty sure he was borderline diabetic). One day I went to him and told him that, if he didn't change, he wasn't going to be around much longer. I actually told him that he needed to stop being a stubborn son of a bitch and think about his family. We needed him around.

With him so focused on his businesses and the stress that comes along with it, being out of shape could have easily led to a heart attack. Something I said resonated with him and he agreed to start making changes. I recommended that he start and commit entirely to the same program that changed my life. He was 50 at the time. In 90 days, my dad became absolutely shredded! Yes, that's right, my 50-year-old dad got a legit six pack. It cracks me up when 35-year-old men tell me they are too old to get a six pack. All I have to do is show my dad's results photos and it shuts them right up.

My mom got involved as well. She wasn't out of shape, but she also didn't really take care of herself. The only reason she wasn't overweight was because she never ate. When she did eat, though, it wasn't good quality food. But mom committed along with Dad and got outstanding results as well. She even took it a step further. At the age of 53, she decided to participate in a bodybuilding competition. I kid you not, she was one of the most shredded women on stage and even placed in the top 20! I'm sorry, but my parents prove that your "I'm too old to work out" excuse is invalid.

Working out isn't the only time people use the "I'm too old" excuse. Building a business is another. Many people of all ages come to me wanting to build a fitness business. There have been quite a few times when I have heard the "I'm too old" excuse. At that point, I like to explain that what they are saying to me is in fact an excuse, nothing more. Their limited way of thinking is limiting their potential. Think about this for a minute. Colonel Harland David Sanders (yes, Colonel Sanders) started KFC when he was 65 years old. Ray Kroc founded McDonald's at the age of 52. John Pemberton founded Coca Cola at the age of 55. I believe those men did pretty well for themselves. Age is just a number. You're never too old to start.

'I'm too young'

On the flip side, many people say they are "too young." This I hear a lot when it comes to starting a business. A lot of young people have incredible minds and come up with some absolutely fantastic business ideas. However, most get in their own way. They believe that being young doesn't allow them to start and effectively grow a business. Somewhere along the way, someone probably told them that they would never be able to accomplish something because of their age. That's just not true. They might not have wisdom and experience on their side just yet, but they can always work hard and learn as they go. Wisdom and experience come with time.

I started my business at the age of 22. Do you know how many people doubted that I would be able to be successful with it because of my age? Too many. Was I clueless about what I was doing? Sure, I'll admit that, but it never stopped me from pushing hard daily. Through an incredible amount of research and hard work, I was able to figure it out. If I had listened to those who told me I was "too young" to build a successful business, I wouldn't be writing this book. Once again, age is just a number.

"I don't know enough'

There are so many people who want to know everything before they start something. That's not possible! You're not going to be able to learn everything there is to know about nutrition before you make a change to your health. I've been in the health and fitness industry since 2008 and I'm still learning daily and will continue to learn for years to come. I always take a "start now, learn as you go" approach. It's an approach that you should adopt as well.

When you married your spouse, did you know everything there is to know about keeping your relationship strong, raising kids, and how to communicate and express feelings? Of course you didn't! But that didn't stop you from marrying your spouse, did it? Of course not. You will learn all of these things over time as you go through your marriage journey together.

It's no different with a business opportunity. It could be the greatest opportunity in history, but some people will still have to know everything before pulling the trigger and getting involved. They research and research and then eventually decide that, because they don't know enough, it's not for them. Do you think I knew everything about my business when I joined? Good lord, no. I was basically jumping in blindly! That turned out pretty well because I decided to just take action and learn later. Even to this day I'm still learning something new every day.

I want you to look at it this way. One day I woke up and decided to write this book. I was not an author. I had no experience with writing a book. I had no idea what the structure should be. I was clueless about what I needed to do to publish the book. I wasn't sure what was supposed to go on the back cover. I wasn't even sure what the front cover would look like. But yet, even with the little knowledge I had, I still fired up my computer and started writing. I took action. I didn't wait, I just started. I knew the moment I opened the computer that it would be a journey, but I would eventually learn everything I needed to know in order to publish an incredible book.

Take action. Don't Wait. Just Start.

Don't wait for the perfect time to start. There is no such thing as a perfect time. You're not going to be able to learn everything there is to know beforehand. Does that mean that you shouldn't do your research before you do something? Of course not! You can prepare and learn enough to make a decision, but don't let lack of knowledge ever stop you from doing something if you feel like it's the right opportunity. Close your eyes and jump right in! You will learn as you go.

STEP 2: ELIMINATING NEGATIVE THOUGHTS

Each of us has the ability to control and manipulate our thoughts. I want you to take a minute and do a little exercise. I'm a car guy and maybe you are too. If not, that's fine too. Just play along. I want you to picture yourself in the driver's seat of the car of your dreams. Think about the color of the exterior, wheels, and interior. There is not a speck of dust or dirt on the car because it's never been driven before. It's so shiny that you can see a perfect reflection of yourself in the paint. You open the door and the smell of new leather hits you in the face. You then sit down in the driver's seat and the seat hugs you.

You look ahead and realize you're on a long runway with no planes, people, or other cars around. It's just you and your car. It's 72 degrees, there's not a cloud in the sky and the sun is shining through the windshield and warming your body. You turn your hat backwards and put on your shades. You push the start engine button and hear the roar of the exhaust. It's a low, mean growl. You rev up the engine a few times and hear nothing but raw power. You grip tightly with one hand on the leather wrapped wheel and press down firmly on the gas pedal. The tires spin for a fraction of a second, but then grip the pavement and you are flown back into your seat. In 2.5 seconds, you reach 60 MPH, then 100, then 150, then 200. You can feel the adrenaline surge throughout your body. Your heart is racing, and you have the biggest smile on your face.

OK now snap out of it. What did you see? How did you feel? If you actually did the exercise, you created every moment in your mind with precision. You could actually see yourself there, smell the aromas in the air, and feel a true sense of adrenaline and happiness. If you're a car guy, you probably feel pretty damn good right now. You just had 100% control of your thoughts and the ability to manipulate them in an instant.

But now I'm going to make you feel a little uncomfortable. I want you to think about a bad experience from your past. Maybe it's when a bully picked on you. Maybe you found yourself in some serious trouble with the law. Maybe you let someone down who's very close to you. Take a second and actually picture that moment in your mind. Think about how you felt, what you went through. Suddenly, your mood and demeanor has changed and a little bit of anxiety, sadness, or anger might have set in, right? Right now, I'm thinking about that moment in school when a group of bullies followed me into the bathroom and pushed me into the urinal causing me to piss all over my sweatshirt. I am thinking about how embarrassed I felt, how self-conscious I was, how much I was defeated and scared. I'm remembering all of the students laughing at me and whispering about me when I got back to the classroom. It's not a good feeling. I went from a feeling of happiness and positivity while thinking about going 200 MPH in my dream car to sadness and negativity in an absolute instant. That only happened, though, because I allowed it to happen. I formulated each of these thoughts in my mind. In an instant, I changed how I felt by what I was thinking.

Your mind can be your biggest asset or your biggest enemy. Whichever one it is has to do with your ability to control your thoughts. If you're analytical like me, your mind can be especially detrimental to your mental state if you allow negative thoughts to thrive and consume your mind. It happened to me quite often when I was young being bullied and it even began to happen again as I tried to figure out why I was battling Lyme in 2015.

Being analytical over negative things leads to worrying and worrying leads to stress and anxiety. Even if you don't have an analytical personality, worrying is fairly common. Worrying can quickly spiral out of control, though. Once you begin to worry, it's very hard to stop worrying. Now you can begin to understand why severe anxiety, panic attacks, and depression set in for many people. Their negative thoughts lead them down that path. Instead of having positive thoughts, they dwell on the negative ones. Dwell on the negative for long and it eventually becomes habit. It's never good when negative thinking becomes a part of who you are. If people just understood the power they have over their thoughts and mental state, they could easily reverse the depression and stop the anxiety.

Again, the problem is that once you begin thinking negatively, it's very hard to stop. Negativity is like cancer, it spreads and spreads until it fills the entire body. It's like a darkness that you can feel at your core. Eventually the negativity gets so bad that you feel like you've lost all control. Sometimes you feel like you're at the bottom of a deep, dark well looking up at the tiny bit of light shining in through the surface, but with no way of climbing up the well. You feel totally trapped. But you're not. You can escape. That negativity can be destroyed. It takes an incredible amount of effort, time, and energy, but it can be done. It involves slowly replacing those negative thoughts with positive ones and developing a habit of doing so. For example, as soon as you begin to think about the negative experience in the exercise I had you do, instantly stop your thoughts and replace that negativity with the positive experience of going 200 MPH in your dream car. From this point on, whenever you start thinking about something negative, stop yourself and replace it with a thought that makes you happy. Those happy thoughts can consist of anything that's going well in your life. Or it can be something that doesn't directly involve you, but makes you feel good. That's the goal, to make you feel good, to make you feel happy.

When self-doubt consumes your mind, consciously replace that doubt with belief. If you are going in for an interview for a job and think you're going to mess up, stop and think about how you're going to crush it! Every single person has the power to manipulate their thoughts in this way. Once you understand it and fill your mind with positivity on a daily basis, your mind becomes free of the prison you feel you have been trapped in for so long. But again, this takes time, sometimes a lot of it depending on how deeply rooted negativity is in your mindset. Every day, consciously stop yourself from the negative thoughts and replace them with positive ones. Over time you will become a new person, one with newfound confidence and happiness.

Let me elaborate on something for a minute. I talked a lot in the previous paragraph about being conscious of your thoughts. What exactly does this mean? When thoughts run through our minds every day, we tend to not think about them. Strange thing to say, I know, but it's true. They just happen. That's fine if they are positive thoughts, but not so much when they are negative. When we are trying to work hard to change our mindset and replace negative thoughts with positive ones, we have to be constantly aware that the negative thoughts are actually occurring. So, what we do is train ourselves to stop and think about our thoughts. When we are consciously aware of our negativity, only then can we stop ourselves and replace it with positivity. One way to do so is to journal your thoughts. Anytime you catch yourself thinking negatively, I want you to write it down. This will teach you to actually be aware of what you're thinking. Once you become aware, then you can start to replace with positive thoughts. Make sense?

If you're someone suffering from anxiety, this is crucial. When I was going through that dark time dealing with Lyme disease and developed awful anxiety, I never took the time to stop and think about what I was getting so worked up about. I just let the anxiety happen. After reading through some books about dealing with anxiety, especially when it came to illness, I learned I had to pause each time I became anxious and think about exactly what was causing me to be anxious. When I thought about it, I quickly discovered there was absolutely no merit for me getting so worked up. The only thing causing the anxiety was the worrying! That's it, nothing more, nothing less. Just the worrying.

For example, there were many times during my treatment that I relapsed badly, meaning all of my symptoms returned and I became very sick again. Once that happened, I instantly developed anxiety and started worrying about never being able to heal. That anxiety quickly turned into a full-blown panic attack where my heart and mind started racing. Once I learned how to properly handle it, the moment I started feeling just a wee bit anxious, I stopped my thoughts entirely and analyzed the situation. What I discovered was that the anxiety only stemmed from my fear of not healing, that's it. I was getting worked up over something I couldn't immediately control. I was getting worked up over a fear of something that probably wouldn't happen!

Once I stopped and fully understood the situation, I could calm myself. Over time, being conscious of my thoughts allowed me to get the anxiety under control. Does that mean that I am anxiety free? For the most part, but there are moments that arise in my daily living that bring back memories of the illness and those awful panic attacks. When that happens, my mind wants to instantly go back to that place. But again, I become conscious of what is happening and get it under control. This is me being very real with you guys. I struggle just like you do.

Positive thinking has been a big part of my life for a long time. I truly feel there is nothing I can't do. However, that doesn't mean that negativity doesn't creep in from time to time because it does. There are going to be moments when negativity and anxiety want to return. Maybe you experience a setback at work or get into a terrible argument with your spouse. It's bound to happen. There's nothing you can do to hide from it and you most certainly can't run from it. The negativity will somehow crawl its way back into your mind, because that pathway in the mind is familiar, well-trodden. Once again, you must be consciously aware of it. If you are, you can easily shake it and get back to your positive self. But if you slowly let it control your mind, you can easily find yourself in that dark place once again. You have to constantly work on your mindset! Maybe this book will be that go-to for you when you do have negativity creep back into your life. For me it's

The Magic of Thinking Big. Do whatever you have to do to get your mind in the right place.

Step 3: Handling Failure

I want you to put yourself in this scenario and then select the option that best describes how you would normally handle the situation.

Let's say you start your own side business because you feel you have so much more potential than working for 16 hours a day at a job you don't enjoy for the rest of your life. You also have found yourself in a tough financial position and really need the extra money that this side business would bring.

Getting your business off the ground has been tough, though. You have no experience as a business owner and face a challenging learning curve. To make it worse, you don't really have any guidance from anyone, so you must learn everything on your own. A few months in, you start making about a hundred bucks a week, but then you hit a plateau lasting another four months. You just can't figure out what you need to do to make it work! Then your paycheck starts decreasing. Week by week you make less and less to the point where you receive a $6 check. You have been relying on this paycheck coming in each week to make ends meet. Making so little means that you might not be able to make your car payment next month.

Based on how you've handled similar situations like this in your past, what would be your next step?

A: Begin to think that this business might not be for you. You get frustrated that you can't make it work and start blaming it on the fact that you've not had any guidance to this point.

After taking time to think about it, you can't justify working several hours a day after already working 16 hours with your day job and not seeing any progress. It just makes sense for you to accept that this isn't for you and just quit and move on to something else.

B: You have a moment of frustration, but not because you don't feel this opportunity is the right one for you, but because you know you're not living up to your potential. However, you take a deep breath, calm yourself down, and start thinking about the reasons why your paycheck has steadily decreased. You write down those reasons and then start coming up with adjustments you can make so that you can start moving forward again. The next day you start applying those changes to your business.

If you chose option B, obviously you're correct. What's funny is that most of you are sitting there proud that you chose the right option, but deep down inside know that your past decisions would have led you to choose option A. Don't fool yourself! It's OK if you chose option A. Now you have to acknowledge that you made the wrong choice. That's good. That's what I want. Only when you admit to yourself that you've been making mistakes can you start to correct course and make progress.

That scenario above is the exact one I faced when I was eight months into my business. The majority of people would have given up. I know that to be true because I witness similar situations on a weekly basis with those on my team. The moment they come across their first major obstacle, they tend to get frustrated, blame someone or something else, and pull back from the business. Because of the frustration and lack of effort, their business eventually completely fails, and they quit. That's not how I'm geared, though. I accepted that I failed, didn't get too upset about it, analyzed what I did wrong, figured out what adjustments to make, and immediately took action so that I could move forward again. That was a big turning point for my business.

How you handle failure has everything to do with your ability or inability to succeed. I've failed multiple times in my business. I failed multiple times during my long baseball career. I've failed with certain areas of my marriage. I've failed with my health. But here I am writing a book about success in all of these areas. It's got a lot to do with how I'm able to handle each failure. Teaching you the exact process I use can help you go from continuously struggling in all aspects of your life to finding success. It really is that simple. Most people have the complete wrong approach to failure. They get frustrated, make excuses, blame someone or something else, and then give up. Not me and not you anymore. Just a few tweaks to your process and things will instantly change. There is a 5-step process that I use that I want to teach to you.

Step 1: Embrace failure and accept responsibility. This is key. Failure happens and you have to expect it and no longer get frustrated when it arrives. Rather, you need to embrace it, realize that it's a part of your journey and your failure is nobody's fault but your own. Stop blaming others for your mistakes! I know it's easy to do because it makes you feel somewhat better convincing yourself that you're not to blame, but deep down inside you know damn well it's your own fault. It always is. Did I blame the government for us having to use food stamps? Of course I didn't. That would be ridiculous. It wasn't the government's fault we were in the situation we were in; it was my own. In that moment in the grocery store, I realized I had failed my family and took full responsibility for it.

Example: Let's say you just started your own side business and were so close to getting your first client, but the person backed out at the last minute and now they are ignoring every phone call. Instead of getting frustrated and blaming something else for your issue, embrace that somewhere you messed up. Something you said or did has caused you to lose that potential client. It's OK, it happens to everyone. Don't let one little setback ruin any chance you have to move forward in the business.

Step 2: Write down what you failed with and why you believe you failed. Dig hard for the answer. When you know exactly what you failed at and why you failed, then can you work to find a solution.

Example: In the same situation above, you would write down that you lost the client and why you think that happened. After going through and analyzing your communication with the prospect, maybe you conclude that you came across as too "salesy." You came across as someone out to benefit you, not them.

Step 3: Figure out and write down a solution. Take some time (not too much time) to think about what you can change so you don't continue to fail with the same thing again. Once you figure it out, write down your solution to the problem.

Example: In the same situation, you realized that you needed to relax a bit (since you are so new) and go into much more detail about the value of what you have to offer. Once you make those changes, you believe you can get the person to purchase from you.

Step 4: Seek help from someone who knows more about the subject than you. Once you have your solution written down, go to a mentor and ask if they feel your solution is the proper solution. Maybe they have experienced that failure before and can guide you in the right direction. If they haven't experienced it before, but they might be able to brainstorm with you and offer ideas to figure out a better solution. If you don't have access to a mentor, go online and do some research.

Example: Your father, also a business owner, has been in similar situations before, so you talk to him about your problem and proposed solution. He agrees with your solution, but also suggests that you spend more time developing a relationship with your potential client.

Step 5: Immediately take action! Too many people go through steps 1-4, but never do step 5. Taking action is the most important part of this process. Once you figure out the proper solution to your failure, you have to apply that solution immediately. It's important that you don't procrastinate with this step. The longer you wait, the greater the chance you're going to forget about your solution and never apply it.

Example: You take your solution and your father's proposed adjustments and apply them to the next person you talk to.

That 5-step process is one I've been using for a lot of years, pretty much since I was 15 years old. Using that process day-in and day-out with every little obstacle and failure you come across will change your life. I can just about guarantee it. Don't settle for external excuses; search for internal improvements. The great thing is that it's not difficult to do. It just involves you shifting your mindset and thinking about things just a little bit differently. But then again, you have to get to the point where the process is engraved in your mindset. If you are someone who is used to coming up with excuses, blaming others, getting frustrated with setbacks, this is going to be a major change.

At first, every inch of your brain will want to reject the process. Negative thinking is like an addiction. Once you stop, it just wants to keep coming back, especially during the initial stages of making changes. It's because it's something that you're so used to doing, and the mind wants to automatically go back to that familiar place. You can't allow that to happen. But thinking positively, constantly for weeks will eventually break the habit. Then the new habit will form, one that actually helps you move forward.

One of my favorite subjects to talk about when speaking at events is overcoming failure. When I'm speaking about overcoming failure, one example I enjoy using has to do with snowboarding. Snowboarding isn't easy to learn. Just ask anyone. They will tell you that it's one of the toughest, most frustrating sports to grasp. You need a ridiculous amount of patience and mental strength just to be able to get good enough to stay up on the board the entire way down the hill. There are so many lessons to be learned from the process of learning to snowboard and I'm about to share a story with you right now.

I've been snowboarding for a lot of years. The process of learning how to do so was challenging to say the least. When I got good enough, though, I started teaching others how to snowboard. I will never forget teaching one of my good friends, Adam. Adam's process of learning is a perfect example of the proper way to handle failure.

Adam is one of those unique people with the ability to quickly get out of his own way, listen, study others, analyze, and make quick adjustments so that he's able to consistently move forward in life. When I started teaching him, I knew he would pick it up quickly, but I didn't realize he would pick it up *that* quickly. He was by far the fastest person I've ever witnessed to learn how to snowboard!

The first time up the mountain, he couldn't stop falling every few feet, which is normal. Even though I was teaching him how to stand up on the board and ride the back edge, it's another thing to actually do it yourself. It takes time and patience to fully grasp the concept. He fell down, got back up, tried again, and repeated the process for an hour or so. I followed him closely down the hill, constantly offering advice to correct anything he was doing wrong. Every single time I offered the advice, he listened and made adjustments. He asked a lot of questions as well, which is an important process in mastering anything. After a lot of falling down, getting back up, and adjusting, it just clicked for him. Within a few hours, he was able to ride down the mountain, swiftly shifting from riding straight to his back edge, while only falling a few times.

Every time we went back up the mountain, he got better and better. Not only was he watching how I rode, listening to my advice, he was watching others as well. In addition, he was learning from his own mistakes and adjusting faster than anyone I've ever witnessed before. Then, after he got a good feel for riding the back edge, it was time to learn how to move to the front edge. It was difficult for him at first, but his process of falling (failing), analyzing, and adjusting repeatedly, quickly allowed him to shift from his back to front edge with ease. By the end of day 1, he was capable of riding down the entire mountain without falling. I kept telling him how amazing it was to experience his ability to learn so quickly.

Take note of Adam's process. He didn't hop on the board for the first time, fall on his ass, and then say, "Well, this sucks. It must not be for me," blame it on the board, and quit. Rather, he understood failing as just a part of the process of becoming a good rider. Each time he fell, he stopped to think about exactly why he fell, watched others, asked me for advice, and made quick adjustments. That is the only reason he was able to learn how to snowboard so quickly.

What about failure as it pertains to health and fitness? I think this is important to address, since obviously health is a major topic I cover in this book. You're going to take the same 5-step process and apply it to your health journey as well. For example, let's say that your weight loss has come to a halt after 4 months of working hard. Instead of getting frustrated about it, expect that plateaus will occur. Take responsibility that something you're doing isn't working. Then take a step back and look at the possible culprits of the plateau. You figure out that there are two possible reasons. First, you might be eating too many calories. Second, you might be overtraining. After talking to a fitness coach, you both conclude that you're simply eating too much. Then you make the necessary adjustments and continue to see results once again.

One last example of the importance of failure and adjustments. Look at success like a boxing match between two equally talented boxers. Sometimes a fighter has to go all 12 rounds to win the match. In those 12 rounds, the fighters beat the living hell out of each other, especially in the early rounds. After the bell rings for each round, the fighters go back to their respective corners and discuss with their trainers what adjustments they need to make for the next round. Each adjustment is based off of something each fighter was struggling with (failure) during the previous round or a weakness they discovered in their opponent. The one who ends up winning the fight normally is the one who makes the best adjustments. Every single fighter goes into the match with a plan. But in order to win, that plan has to change multiple times based on obstacles experienced during the actual fight. Succeeding in business, fitness, or relationships is just a long, drawn-out boxing match. The punches you take are the obstacles and failures you come across, and you have to quickly adjust each time if you want to be crowned the winner.

So, to wrap it all up, use my 5-step failure process with all aspects of your life. Boom. Next section.

STEP 4: CONQUERING FEAR

Fear controls most people's lives. Fear of the past. Fear of the future. Fear of the unknown. Fear of change. Fear of public speaking. Fear of failure. Fear of heights. Fear of spiders. Fear of judgment. Fear of bellybuttons. Yes, I'm being serious. My wife Melinda has a fear of bellybuttons and it's called omphalophobia. I just discovered that actually while writing this and I'm basically pissing my pants laughing so hard! But there's basically a fear for everything.

Fear is debilitating, something that holds people back from succeeding and causes a lot of unnecessary anxiety and stress. One of my favorite bands of all time, Shinedown, has a phrase in their song "Get Out" that says, "hard to move mountains when you're paralyzed." Basically, what they mean is that you can never achieve your full potential if you don't move. Most people can't move because of fear. It's paralyzing.

Imagine this. Everyone has a bubble that surrounds them. Inside that bubble is called the "comfort zone." Picture a giant bubble with the most comfortable, badass recliner in the middle of it. Normal, everyday activities are done within that comfort zone. Most people almost never venture outside that bubble because fear traps them inside. Sometimes, though, an opportunity comes along to improve their life in some way, they get motivated, and decide that today is the day they are going to break through that comfort zone. Once they stick their toe out, though, the fear of failure, rejection, and change (picture big ass monsters with large teeth) start coming at them full force. They become scared shitless and pull that toe back in to feel safe once again. That person let those fears hold them back from possibly experiencing something life-changing! This is the majority of people.

But then, every once in a while, you come across someone like me. The way I think and act is not normal. But people like me start with a bubble and then quickly realize that the bubble just keeps them trapped in an average lifestyle. I don't want to be average in any aspect of my life. I always have to be getting better and better with everything I do. Sitting on that recliner in the middle of that bubble every day doesn't allow me to do so. So, what we do is take a knife and destroy the bubble. Those fears still come at us at full force, but we no longer have a bubble to protect us, so we face those fears like a boss!

What we quickly come to discover, though, is that none of those fears can actually physically harm us. They are there, but they can only get in our face and growl at us. They can intimidate us and play mind games, but they can't hurt us. They were only scary because we believed they were scary. Eventually we learn that, since they can't actually hurt us, they aren't that scary after all. Then those fears just disappear entirely.

Let's take someone with a fear of heights. The majority of people with that fear will always stay on the ground. They won't fly on planes, won't go skiing, won't go off high diving boards, and sure as hell won't go skydiving. Their fear is just too overwhelming and makes them overly uncomfortable. Every time they even begin to think about heights it scares them to death! Their heart rate increases, palms become sweaty, and anxiety takes over. They refuse to put themselves in a situation that involves heights.

Successful people, though, have a much different approach. They understand that the only way to conquer fear is by doing the thing they fear most. Even if they fear heights, they will be the first to venture to the top of that ski mountain or jump out of the plane. Will their heart race a little? Absolutely. Will they be uncomfortable doing it? For sure. What happens, though, is that once they jump out of that plane, they quickly realize the fear itself was the only scary part. 99.9% of the time, nothing terrible will happen. Over time, constantly facing that fear will evaporate the fear itself.

Fear of public speaking

Do you have a fear of public speaking? More than likely you do. Believe it or not, people fear public speaking more than they fear death and that's why it's the first fear I'm addressing. In the past, one of my biggest fears was public speaking. I absolutely hated it with a passion. Whenever I was asked to present in front of the class, I would shake and get myself so worked up that I would forget what I was saying. Because of being bullied, I feared judgment and being laughed at. I would get in front of the class, look out to the other students and think about the nasty things they were probably thinking about me. I could never really focus on the topic because my fear overwhelmed me. I became so stressed out that, afterward, I would literally develop some sort of illness. I'm not talking about puking from the nerves; I'm talking about getting the flu, mono, or something else. The insane amount of stress I put on myself before and during the presentation must have always severely weakened my immune system. This happened just about every time.

Once I started my own business, though, I understood that I had to force myself to do the thing I feared most, to get on stage and present to a large group of people. I remember a business training event held in Columbus, OH back in 2009. At the event, a lot of successful fitness coaches went on stage to speak about success, but there were also people who volunteered to get up and share their story as well. As much as I didn't want to, I volunteered to be one of those people because I knew that if I didn't face my fear I would never be able to conquer it. I instantly regretted that decision. I remember sitting nervously in my chair in the front row, fidgeting, and reciting in my head over and over again what I would say when I got on stage. My heart raced and by the time my name was called to go on stage, I was pretty sure I was going to puke. I walked up the stage and looked out to the crowd of over 250 people, all eyes glaring at me, and I about shit my pants! 250 people. That's a lot of people.

I wish I could have seen myself because I'm sure I looked like a deer caught in headlights. I fumbled on my words, forgot a few things I was going to say, but did it. When I finished my story, I heard the applause and got the hell off that stage. After the event, I had some time to reflect and realized that it wasn't nearly as bad as I thought it was going to be. Sure, I sucked, but I got through it. I quickly began to understand that my fear was far worse than actually being on stage and speaking.

At the next event, I volunteered again. I was still nervous, but not as nervous as the previous time. For a few years, I volunteered to get up and speak at every event I possibly could. Each time I spoke, the more comfortable I became and the better I got. Eventually, after about 5 years, it got to the point where I could speak to a crowd of 1,000 people like they were my best friends. I no longer got nervous. I actually thoroughly enjoyed being on stage. Then people started inviting me to speak at their events and, of course, I gladly accepted.

Now public speaking is something I am very passionate about and love doing. I will take time out any day of the week to speak to people about something I'm passionate about if the opportunity come up. One of my future goals is to become a public speaker. That's how much I enjoy doing it!

I want to take this a little further and give you some sound tips to help you become a better speaker. I realize that the fear of public speaking is common. Here are 7 tips on how to conquer the fear and become a better public speaker.

1. **Repetition.** If you want to get over your fear of speaking in front of others, you must force yourself to get out and speak in front of others. This is the only way to overcome the fear. The first time won't be enjoyable, but just as I did, you will quickly understand that your actual fear is the worst part of it all. Being on stage really isn't all that bad. The more you do it, the more comfortable you will become.

2. **Knowledge.** Have a good grasp of what you're going to present. I've witnessed a lot of cringeworthy presentations over the years because people decided to go on stage without fully understanding what they actually meant to talk about. That's the wrong approach. Do your research. When you are knowledgeable about the subject you're presenting on, you tend to have more confidence. The more confidence you have, the better you present.

3. **Have a plan.** Don't hop on stage and expect to "wing it" and crush the presentation. In my experience, those who "wing it" are all over the place with their presentation and confuse the audience. Personally, I like to write down bullet points on a small piece of paper, stick it in my pocket and bring it up on stage. Normally, I memorize the bullet points so I don't have to bring out the paper, but occasionally I do have to bring it out so that I can stay on

track. Another mistake that people will make is that they will literally write down and read their entire speech. You don't want to read on stage. Reading shows the audience that you aren't confident in what you're talking about and didn't properly prepare. Plus, reading is incredibly boring and lacks emotion. You don't want to bore your audience.

4. **Believe in yourself.** This is a very hard one for those who deal with an intense fear of public speaking, but it's crucial to a successful speech. When you believe in yourself, others tend to believe in you as well. The worst thing that you can do right before heading on stage is have a moment of self-doubt. That will lead to anxiety and then the domino effect and not in a good way. I talked a lot already about replacing negative thoughts with positive ones. Right before you head on stage is a good time to throw those negative, self-diminishing thoughts out of your head and replace them with positive, self-esteem boosting thoughts. That would be a good time to stop for a minute, relax, and tell yourself that you are going to crush the presentation! There is nothing wrong with saying things in your head like "I'm a badass!" and "I know I can do this!" The more positive the thoughts, the more relaxed you will be on stage and the better you will present. One other additional tip I can give you is to bring your favorite self-help book with you, such as this book (wink) or *The Magic of Thinking Big*, mark a page that really boosts your self-confidence, and read it 15 minutes before heading on stage.

5. **Be passionate!** The best speakers I have ever heard are insanely passionate about what they are talking about. Have you ever heard Tony Robbins speak? If you haven't, you need to. It doesn't matter what the hell he's talking about, his passion is absolutely contagious! You can't help but listen to what he's saying and get pumped up because

he's so pumped up. So, don't ever present on something that you're not passionate about. That would be like me trying to present about fashion. That would make no sense.

6. **Breathe**. Most of the time people just forget to breathe. There is a breathing exercise that I like to do that relaxes me in stressful situations. In the past, right before going on stage, my mind would race, but I took a few minutes to clear my mind completely. After clearing your mind, take five slow, deep breaths, breathing in through your nose and out through your mouth. On the fifth breath, hold it for ten seconds and then slowly breathe out. This should calm you down right before heading on stage.

7. **Smile**. Have you ever been to a good presentation from a professional and not seen him/her smile? Yeah, me neither. It's cliché, but smiling is contagious. You want the audience to feel happy, so smile. In addition, smiling causes you to be happy as well. When everyone is happy, all is good.

Fear of change

The majority of people don't like to change. In their minds, it's easier to stay in that recliner than to venture out of the bubble and feel uncomfortable. What's ironic about the situation, though, is that they only think they are comfortable because they have been camped out in that bubble for years. It doesn't matter how terrible their situation may be, to them it's much easier to stay put than to make a change. They fear making a change, but don't realize that once they actually do make a change, they will become far more comfortable and happier than they ever were inside the bubble.

Take someone who is 200 lbs. overweight, for example. For years and years, they have been stuck inside their comfort zone with absolutely terrible habits. They have used food to cope for so long that it's become a lifestyle they are used to. It's comfortable to them. They know deep down inside that they need to change, but the fear of actually making the change keeps them planted safe and warm inside that bubble. If they do decide to change, will it be hard? Well yeah, of course it will. It will be the hardest thing they ever do in their life! But if they get over the fear and commit to change, over time they will lose the weight and discover a new, healthier lifestyle that feels a hell of a lot better than their old lifestyle. But first, they have to get over that fear of changing. If you are someone in this situation, I want you to think about this. The temporary feeling of being uncomfortable is far better than permanent death. I know it's a daunting task to make such a massive change in your life, but your life depends on it! If you want to talk about it, I'm here to help.

Here's another example. When I'm teaching others how to snow-board, one thing I notice in a lot of beginner snowboarders is their fear to move to the next level of difficulty on the slopes. For example, they start out on a Green, the easiest route, but have a hard time making the transition to a Blue, which is one level up in difficulty. It's not that they can't do it because they have all the skills to do so, but the fear holds them back. Once again, they fear change. I know a lot of people who stay on Greens for years because they fear the Blues. The transition from Blues to Blacks takes even longer.

However, I have also taught other guys who are practically fearless and constantly push outside their comfort zone. These guys might not even have the skills yet, but they will move from Greens to Blues to Blacks within the first year (or sooner) on the slopes. Sure, they take some nasty falls along the way, but they understand that the only way to get better is by consistently challenging themselves and overcoming their fear. They don't fear change, they embrace it. You also have to learn to embrace change.

Fear of judgment

Do you fear judgment from others? Probably. The amount of people who care what others think is more than you can imagine. I know this from personal experience after working with so many people over the years. Many times, that fear will stop someone dead in their tracks from making a change. With me being a fitness coach, I see it quite often with my clients. You'd be surprised how vicious friends and family (and others) can be when you attempt to make a change with your health. The thought of being ridiculed, laughed at, being told that you will never succeed is more than enough to cause people to abandon their plans and continue on an unhealthy path.

Many of my clients come to me for advice about their experiences with people who are close to them. Most of the time it has to do with the lack of support at home regarding nutrition. It's common that they get ridiculed for eating something healthy. This happened to me constantly when I first began to make changes in 2008. People constantly rubbed in my face the fact that they were eating pizza while I was eating something healthier. Often, they would make comments and then tempt me with a slice of pizza on my plate. It wasn't particularly enjoyable, but I always stayed strong. This type of situation is very common with those who begin to make positive changes in their health.

But why? Why do people seem to judge and ridicule you about a shift to a healthy lifestyle? It has everything to do with how uncomfortable you make them feel when you begin to make changes. When you make a positive change in your life, especially with your health, they know you are doing what is best for you and making good choices. They know that it's something you need to do. But if they are making poor choices themselves, your good choices tend to make them feel guilty that they are not making the same changes. Deep down inside they know they need to make the same change, but aren't for whatever reason. The thought of change scares the hell out of them. So instead of supporting you, they would rather judge you, tear you down, or get upset with you. They want the "old you" back because the "new you" threatens their current lifestyle. They want to be able to continue living in a "comfortable" state on an unhealthy path with you by their side.

This is especially true when one spouse makes a change and the other doesn't. I've seen this cause more issues in a marriage than I can count! They don't want to eat separate meals or listen to and see you work out every day. Every time they do, they feel like a ton of bricks drops on their shoulders. As each day passes and you make more and more changes, the more the guilt sets in about not taking the same approach with their own health. Plus, they fear losing you or that you will become a totally different person. It's much easier to tear you down and try to get you to give up and revert back to the old lifestyle than step outside their comfort zone and make a change. Once they "get you back," they no longer experience that guilt, so they may try damn hard to get you to revert to your old lifestyle.

However, good friends and family eventually understand why you are making the changes and support you. Sometimes it takes a while, but if you talk to them, explain how much this means to you, they will come around. If they still don't support you, they are assholes. That's just the straight up honest truth. If your spouse doesn't support you when you're trying to do something positive for yourself and others, they aren't a good spouse. If they do support you, though, there's a great chance you might be able to get them on board with this new lifestyle. I've seen it before and have even experienced it myself.

After my family saw me make incredible changes, they became curious and wanted to make changes themselves. This is ideal, especially if everyone lives together, because then everyone is on the same page moving in the same direction. Dinners are no longer awkward, but rather enjoyable because you're all eating the same things and nobody is giving anyone else flak. Sometimes it takes you going out of your way and inviting those closest to you to join you on this journey. You'd be surprised by who hops on board with you. But do not fear judgment of those closest to you. If you feel you are doing the right thing, no matter what it's with, don't pay any attention to those who attempt to tear you down. And again, they might come around and fully support and join you.

How about those who tear you down even though you have no personal relationship with them? This is common because of social media. If you are making some sort of positive change in your life, again maybe with your health, and post about it online, it never fails that you will have a few people who make negative comments. My wife and I have both been there before. When I first posted my fitness transformation online, I had multiple people call me ugly and claim that I used steroids or photo-shopped my results. I might be ugly, but I most certainly did not use any drugs or alter my photos in any way. They were just trying to get under my skin. I like to call these people "haters." Haters are everywhere, especially online. You will find a hater in just about every post you come across on social media, especially if that post has something to do with someone making a positive change in their life.

Haters despise seeing you (or anyone) succeed and will do every-thing in their power to suck the life from you. They want you to be miserable because they want you to feel like them. Make no mistake, every single hater that you come across hates their life. You don't go around tearing others down if you don't. Let me ask you something. How many people do you know who have truly been successful who go around on social media tearing others down? None? Me neither. It doesn't happen. Successful people encourage and support others; they don't tear them down or attempt to discredit or belittle their accomplishments.

I wish I could tell you to not fear judgment because you won't face any from others, but that's simply not true. You will face it constantly as you try to improve your life. As you read through this book and make some positive changes in your life, the haters will slowly appear. They don't want to see you be happy and succeed. Once it happens, ignore it. Yes, that's right, don't pay any attention to it. If they say it to you in person, let it go in one ear and out the other and walk away. If they are doing it online, instantly delete it and don't think twice about it. Nothing good will come out of you taking the time to read through what was posted. All that does is generate negative thoughts and emotions. You want positivity in your life and mind.

Unfortunately, this is easier said than done. My wife is a prime example. When she first posted her "before" and "after" photos online, she received some extremely inappropriate and hurtful comments, especially about her stretch marks. Never mind that she just lost a ton of weight and looked absolutely incredible, they focused on her stretch marks. Being her husband, I wanted to hunt down these bastards and beat the living hell out of them, but I had to restrain myself. These comments had a bigtime effect on my wife, though, and made her very self-conscious and beat down her confidence. She didn't know how to handle the haters and their comments. There were many nights she would cry to me because of how hurtful some of the comments were. I had to teach her exactly what I'm teaching you, why these people do what they do and how to react to it. Once she realized that these people have serious issues of their own and started ignoring the comments and messages, it no longer bothered her.

The worst thing that you can do with a hater is respond to their hatefulness. That's exactly what they want. It's just like a bully. I guess it is a bully, really. Once you respond, they win. Once you ignore, you piss them off. Once you keep ignoring, they eventually realize that you're never going to respond so they go bother someone else. The moment you respond, though, they won't let up. They will continue to dig and dig until they beat you down so much that you fall to their level. When you respond and argue with them, nothing you say or do will change their mind. You have to remember that, if they are taking the time to tear you down, they don't want an argument. They just want to know they got to you. Don't allow them to get to you. As much as you want to argue, it's best to stop what you're doing, take a deep breath, and just move on. It's just not worth your time.

Post

Many people let the fear of judgment hold them back from being themselves. One of the greatest pieces of advice that I can give you, which will help in all aspects of your life, especially relationships and business, is to be you. Be original. Stop trying to pretend you're someone you're not. Stop trying to act like someone else. I see this constantly with others. Will there be some people who don't like the "real you?" Absolutely. But who cares? You shouldn't. I don't. Writing this book, and even posting what I do on social media, I'm well aware that not everyone will connect with me or even like what I have to say. Because of it, they may not even like me. I'm OK with that. There will be people I connect with and people I don't. I can't please everyone. You can't either. There are even people who believe that I should dress "more successfully." I will dress how I want to dress. I'm not the type of guy who enjoys wearing a suit. I'm far more comfortable in a t-shirt, ball cap, and jeans. Even when I'm speaking at events, most of the time that's what I'm wearing. Because I don't fear judgment from others, I experience a freedom that's incredibly exhilarating. In addition, I believe I'm able to connect with and relate to more people. I am who I am. You need to be who you truly are deep down inside. Show the world the real you, not some fake version! Once you do, and stop fearing judgment, you're going to feel like you were just set free.

You will always be judged by others. Who...freaking...cares. Don't let the fear of judgment hold you back from moving forward. Come to expect judgment but be sure to respond to it appropriately. Remember the reasons why people judge you and attempt to tear you down. They are just trying to get to you and bring you down to their level.

Fear of the past

There are many people who have experienced a rough past. Maybe they were physically or verbally abused, or maybe they were extremely poor. Maybe they were bullied severely like I was. Maybe they dealt with addiction. Maybe they dealt with some sort of major health issue, such as cancer. Maybe their parents fought all the time. Maybe you have dealt with some or all of these things. What you have to understand, though, is that your past does not determine your future. Again, your past does not determine your future! Many people who have dealt with rough pasts fear the past will repeat itself. Because they are so focused on the past repeating itself, they can never truly live outside it. They are too caught up in the past to create incredible experiences and reach their full potential. Dwelling on the past just creates fear and hesitation. Only when they let go of the past can they actually move forward.

Fear of the past, fear of anything for that matter, creates anxiety. For example, let's say that you got hurt in a past relationship. When you start to date once again, a little voice in your head keeps telling you to be cautious and to remember all that you went through. Any time you find someone you really like, that voice gets louder and louder. You develop anxiety and pull back from the new person you're seeing, which just chases the person away. Even though the same situation probably won't happen again, your fear prevents you from possibly experiencing an incredible relationship. You don't give yourself a chance to be happy again with someone else. In this situation, you have to just let it go. You have to let go of the past!

Now, don't take that to mean forget your past. There's a difference. Never forget the things that happened to you, for the past is a great learning tool. My past is the only reason why I'm writing this book. As you have already found out, my past has molded me into the person I am today and there are some incredible lessons to be learned from it. If I didn't go through what I went through, struggled as much as I did, I wouldn't be where I am today. But if I dwelled on all my terrible past experiences possibly repeating themselves, I'd be a wreck. I would be paralyzed from moving forward.

So, what I'm saying is that you have to let go of the fear of the past repeating itself. You have to destroy that fear completely. Clear your mind of it. If you have to, picture that fear written down on a piece of paper in your head. Then picture yourself grabbing that piece of paper, crumpling it up, and throwing it in the trash. Strange exercise, I know, but it works. Visualizing yourself "throwing away" the fear can help you actually eliminate the fear. Also, be conscious of the fear. Don't let it be something that is buried in the back of your mind that constantly resurfaces. Rather, when you start to feel anxious just a little bit, pause for a second and actually think about why that feeling is there. Recognize that you are becoming anxious because of the fear. Then ask yourself, "Is this really worth me getting anxious over?" The answer is no. It never is. When you become conscious of your fear and anxiety, then you can begin to have power over it. But let the past go. It has no business being in your present or future as anything other than a teacher guiding you toward improvement and excellence.

In the movie "After Earth," Will Smith's character makes an incredible statement about fear. He said, "Fear is not real. The only place that fear can exist is in our thoughts of the future. It is a product of thoughts you create. Do not misunderstand me. Danger is very real. But fear is a choice." Sure, it's from a fictional movie, but this is one of my all-time favorite quotes. If you think about fears, each one comes to fruition only from thoughts you formulate in your mind. My fear of public speaking came from my thought that people would judge me. I dwelled on those thoughts so often that it gave me terrible anxiety, causing me to completely avoid any type of public speaking for years. It wasn't until I tackled those fears head on that I realized that I wasn't getting judged nearly as much as I thought I was. Sure, some people did judge me, but the fear that people would judge me was far worse than actually being judged by others.

The same happened with those who feared moving to the next difficulty on the slopes. In their minds, they probably pictured themselves suffering severe injury when moving from a Green to a Blue. The odds of them actually severely injuring themselves were slim, but the power in that fear blocked them from ever progressing. Little did they know how simple that transition from Green to Blue actually was; their fear prevented them from making that discovery and moving along. Just remember this, always challenge yourself and do your best to tackle your fears head on. Moving forward in life, whether it be with health, business, or your relationships, relies on your ability to burst outside that comfort zone on a daily basis and overcome your fears. Fear is a choice.

Step 5: Eliminating Instant Gratification

We have a major problem in our society. The creation of fast food, smartphones, Amazon Prime, among other things has caused people to adopt an instant gratification mindset. Hungry? Just go to the drive-thru and order a bunch of food that causes cancer and obesity. Want that new computer by tomorrow? Just go to Amazon Prime and select one-day shipping. Want to connect with your high school buddy that you haven't talked to in ten years? Just quickly look him up on Facebook. And if it doesn't happen fast enough, we get very upset about it.

Since it seems that everything anymore is instant, people get the impression that health and fitness, financial, and relationship success is instant as well. It's not. In fact, it's far from it. You need to take any belief you have about instant gratification and eliminate it from your mind if you want any real success. If not, expect frustration and an inability to ever make progress. Everyone seeks that quick fix that absolutely doesn't exist, at least not when it comes to experiencing real success.

Unfortunately, most companies out there recognize that their customers seek instant gratification and market their products accordingly. Being in the fitness industry, it's extremely frustrating to see all the advertisements for products that promise instant results without any work. Such bullshit. Unfortunately, these advertisements are actually effective from a business standpoint because everyone wants fast results without having to lift a finger.

So people buy into these gimmicks and never end up making any changes. Why? Because they don't work. Next time you see an infomercial for a product like this, pause the TV and read the fine print. Almost every time, you will see a disclaimer saying that the person achieved results with the product along with a change in nutrition and commitment to a steady exercise regimen. Well no shit they are going to get results! They are doing what they should be doing by eating right and working out. That's how results come.

Everyone wants fast results with minimal effort. That's why millions of people go out and buy lottery tickets every day. Rather than putting in consistent work to change their financial situation, they toss money into the lottery to get a very, very slim chance at instantly winning "the big one." When I say slim, I'm talking about something like a 1:175,000,000 chance to win. Yes, that's six zeros. To put that into perspective, you have better odds of getting hit by a falling airplane part, being hit by a meteor, being in a plane crash, and being struck by lightning. You don't see many successful people buying lottery tickets, do you? No, you don't.

I could take that money and invest it and, in 30 years, I could be sitting on a profit of tens of thousands of dollars while those who "invested" in the lottery experience a loss of thousands. I'm never looking for instant results. The instant gratification mindset leads to a life of mediocrity. You don't want to be mediocre, do you? You wouldn't be reading this book if you did.

If you want real lasting results, it takes an incredible amount of time, patience, and effort. As a fitness coach, I witness the lack of patience of others on a weekly basis with people trapped in the mindset that just a few days of work will bring results. They might see a little progress in a few days, sure, but it will be minimal. You'd be surprised by how many people get frustrated they aren't ten pounds lighter after working out and eating healthy for two days. Then they come back to me and complain that they didn't get the results they wanted and quickly go back to their old ways. One of the worst things to see as a coach is someone begin their journey, start making progress, and then shift back to their old unhealthy lifestyle because they don't feel they are getting results quickly enough.

This is why I spend quite a bit of time working on mindset with my new clients. If they go into it believing they will reach their goals in a week, they will be right back where they started in no time. But if they start with an understanding that results take time, effort, and consistency, there's a greater chance they will experience long-term success. It's my responsibility to get them mentally prepared for the long journey ahead. If not, I'm not doing my job.

Post

Sometimes, that journey takes years and years, depending on how much weight they have to lose. As I've said, I've worked with quite a few very obese people and when I say "very obese," I mean they have hundreds of pounds to lose. They are the toughest to work with because instant gratification was a big factor in why they became obese and is completely engraved into their thinking. Food was their escape. Every time they ate something that was bad for them, they felt good. They focused on how good it tasted and how great it made them feel, not the effect on their bodies long term. Over time, the weight slowly piled on. Changing that way of thinking requires a journey of its own. Sometimes outside help is necessary, such as from a therapist. There's nothing wrong with that. Nobody should ever feel ashamed for seeking professional help. The body cannot heal until the mind does. Once they change their mindset and begin committing to a healthy plan, the weight slowly comes off.

Many people have the same issue of instant gratification with food, to some degree, and that's why many people have trouble maintaining results. They may commit fully for a month or two and get pretty outstanding results, but then they begin to slide back to bad habits because they feel they have "earned it." Having yourself a cheat meal every now and then is fine, as you will learn more about later, but doing so regularly can be detrimental and trigger old habits or allow them to linger.

Nobody thinks about how they will feel after they eat unhealthy food; they just quickly eat it to experience that instant satisfaction of great taste. If someone has worked hard to get results and eats something they shouldn't eat (that's not a planned cheat meal), regret normally sets in. You never want to regret something you ate. If you're going to eat a planned cheat meal, great, eat it and don't worry about it. But if you're outside your planned cheat meal and your buddy Joe asks you to split a large pizza, don't just do so on a whim.

If you struggle with instant gratification, especially when it comes to food, I want you to follow something that I like to call the 10-second rule. No, I'm not talking about dropping a piece of food on the floor and picking it up within 10 seconds making it all right to eat. That's gross anyway. This is an exercise that I teach my clients that helps them tremendously. Whenever you are about to indulge in something you know you shouldn't have, take 10 seconds to think about how you will feel afterward. Once you take time to actually think about it, you will realize that it's just not worth it. The key here is to feel the regret before deciding to indulge. If you feel regret beforehand, you're more than likely going to make the right decision. Again, though, this is only when you're not having a cheat meal. If you're having a planned cheat meal, shove that food in your mouth and enjoy every bit of it. But the 10-second rule can actually work with just about every decision you make, not just with food. Get into the habit of applying the rule to your life and you're more than likely going to experience a lot of progress.

Let me address instant gratification in a business context. Success in business takes a long time to attain, sometimes a very long time! Most mom-and-pop shops don't even turn a profit in their first five years. Let that sink in for a moment. For five years they are in the red, struggling to make it work. Some of the most successful businesses out there went years and years without making any money. If they had given up in their first year, look at all they would have missed out on. What if I would have quit 8 months in when I struggled greatly with my business? I can't even imagine. Erase the instant gratification mindset when it comes to business.

 Success is a combination of doing the right things on a daily basis over a period of time. Failure is a combination of doing the wrong things on a daily basis over a period of time. Nobody becomes obese overnight. It takes years and years of poor eating habits. You're not going to eat a cheeseburger tonight and wake up tomorrow and say, "Shit, now I'm obese." But if you eat cheeseburgers every day for six months, I can assure you that you will put on some unwanted weight.

On the flip side, if you eat the right things, work out daily, over time you will become and stay healthy. It's the same with finances. Poor spending habits and money management, such as spending more than you have, over time can lead to tens or even hundreds of thousands of dollars of debt. But the right spending habits and money management over time can lead to true wealth! With every aspect of your life, whether it be your health, relationships, business, or finances, you must shed the instant gratification mentality and have patience. That is the only way for you to ever find success.

STEP 6: OVERCOMING LAZINESS

Right now, at this very moment, on a scale of 1-10 (10 being the highest), I want you to rate your work ethic. What's your number? If it's anything below a 9, you've got work to do. If you put a "1," good lord you've *really* got some work to do! But here's reality. Laziness has become common. I can freely talk about this because Melinda and I were in this position. Food stamps are great if used the way they were intended, but it can cause some people to become incredibly lazy. Too many people anymore are looking for handouts and want everything gifted to them without having to work for it. With food stamps, if you're actively working hard to get your head above water like we were, you're doing the right thing. But if you keep using them for a long period of time without attempting to change your situation, shame on you. Even if you aren't on food stamps, if you want to make a change, but don't actually put effort in to make the change, shame on you.

At that point, you are no longer justified in bitching about your situation, but that's what many people do. They bitch about how poor they are while watching six hours of Netflix a night. They bitch about their bad health while eating fast food for every meal. They bitch about their relationship with their spouse while refusing to seek professional help and work on improving the relationship every damn day. I'm tired of watching people be so lazy! I'm sure you are too. By the way, this might be one of those sections where you really don't like me. I'm OK with that. Be angry but focus on why you're getting angry. Is it because it's like I'm speaking right to you and calling you out? Think about it. I only speak the truth. I want you to change, not remain in the situation you've been in for years.

The life I've created is because of my work ethic. Everything I've accomplished is because of my work ethic. Success doesn't happen without hard work. I want you to ask yourself these questions:

1. Are you working as hard you can right now to change your health?

2. Are you working as hard as possible to change your finances?

3. Are you working as hard as you can to improve your relationship with your spouse, kids, and friends?

Seriously, I want you to take the time to think about it because, if you answered "no" to any of those, you're selling yourself short and will struggle to make progress. Some of you may have answered "yes" to all of them, but you aren't being truthful. You are just saying "yes" because you want to feel good about yourself, but in reality, you could be working so much harder. It's easier to play ignorant than to face the truth. You must be willing to do what nobody else will do if you want to succeed. You must be willing to work harder than everyone else if you want to be better than everyone else. You have to be willing to lose sleep, make sacrifices.

By the way, you can't fake a work ethic either. I meet people all the time who tell me they have an incredible work ethic. But once I start following them on social media, I discover they just want others to believe they work hard. You can't have a good work ethic if you talk about getting home from work and watching *HGTV* until you go to bed.

You have to grind. It's a term that I've been using for years to describe the moments where you push hard constantly even when you don't feel like pushing anymore. Are you out of breath during your workouts? Keep grinding. Are you tired and just want to sleep instead of working on your side gig? Keep grinding. Is everyone else around you making it nearly impossible to eat healthy? Keep grinding! Silence that voice in your head that's telling you to quit. Hell, tell it to f*%& off! You've got things to accomplish. You have to grind and grind and grind until you reach your goals. Even then, though, you keep grinding. You need to get into the habit of grinding. Once you understand what you're able to accomplish when you work your ass off every day, you never want to stop. You will become addicted to the hustle and the results it brings.

It's time that you change. Not later, now! Stop being lazy and start working. The great thing about life is that it's never too late to change. You're never too old. You're never too young. No matter how lazy you've been to this point, you can literally at this very moment change everything. I want you to become the hardest worker you know! I want you to outwork me. Wait a minute, let me rephrase that. I want you to *try* to outwork me (good luck). Push yourself to try and top my work ethic. When you put in the hours, make those sacrifices, and do so consistently, everything in your life will change, I guarantee it.

STEP 7: FINDING YOUR FOCUS AND STAYING MOTIVATED

I have a unique ability to stay focused. Or is it really all that unique? I don't think so. I'm not special when it comes to this.

In fact, I believe that anyone can be just as focused as I am. My ability to stay focused and motivated has everything to do with my reasons to start moving towards my goals in the first place. My reasons are so important to me that I have no other option but to stay motivated and focused on accomplishing each goal that I set, whether it be with my health, finances, or relationships. If you come up with the right reasons and constantly remain focused on those reasons, then you, too, will be able to have laser-like focus and stay motivated to reach your own goals.

You already learned my reason, or "why" as I like to call it, for getting out of that tough financial position we were in. I wanted to provide them with total financial freedom and give them the life that they deserved. I no longer wanted to feel like I was failing them. Every day I woke up, I reminded myself of that "why" so that I could stay focused on doing what I had to do that day in order to move towards that goal. That process repeated day in and day out allowed me to eventually reach my goal. I followed the same process with my health when healing from Lyme Disease.

There are two problems that you're probably experiencing. The first problem is that you don't actually take the time to come up with a strong enough "why" with whatever goal you're trying to accomplish. For example, let's say that you want to make a change with your health and lose weight. That's great, of course, but *why* are you making that change? What kind of "why" can you formulate that's powerful enough to keep you focused and motivated long term? Saying that you want to lose 10 lbs. to gain more confidence is a start, but you have to go much deeper than that. Saying that you "want to gain more confidence" is not going to keep you focused for the amount of time that it will take to accomplish that goal. Instead, that "why" should look something like this. "I want to lose 10 lbs. so that I can look in the mirror and finally be proud of the person staring back. I want to lose 10 lbs.

to be a better example for my children by teaching them healthy habits and to never give up on their goals." That's a real "why."

The second problem is that you purposely ignore your "why" so that you won't feel guilty for giving up. People lose focus because they don't purposely think about their "why" on a daily basis. This is why you need to write down your "why" and stick it in multiple places where you will see it throughout the day. This can be on your computer screen, on your bathroom mirror (suggested), on your refrigerator, or even in your car somewhere. This should be the first thing that you see every morning. However, don't just half-ass read it because I said that you need to read it. Actually, take the time to digest it, think about it hard, and bring out those emotions. The emotions are what will keep you focused and motivated.

When you have strong enough reasons to move toward your goals and constantly remind yourself of those reasons on a daily basis, you will be able to stay focused and motivated to reach your goals. Those who lose motivation are the ones who lose sight of their initial reason/s for starting in the first place. With the right "why" and work ethic, there is nothing stopping you from getting where you want to be. Spend some time today developing very strong "whys" and write them down and place them somewhere you will see them daily.

STEP 8: SETTING GOALS

Setting goals is a crucial step in the success process. In my opinion, success doesn't happen without it. However, I treat goal setting a little differently than most people. Most people set big goals and loosely do what think they have to do to move towards those big goals. There's a few problems with this process. First, big goals are normally daunting and discouraging. For example, maybe you are someone that is trying to lose 200 lbs. If you strictly focus on that goal, you're going to get discouraged thinking about how to make that big weight loss a reality. Instead, you need to break down your goal into smaller, more attainable goals.

I'm a big fan of creating daily, weekly, and monthly goals. The first step is to create daily goals. In the same example above, I would help you make small, easy changes to your nutrition that you can do every day. In addition, another one of your daily goals is to complete your workout. If you can focus on accomplishing those small goals daily, it will help you move towards your big goal of losing 200 lbs. However, it seems so much more attainable tackling small chunks at a time rather than focusing on the big, giant goal.

Next, we focus on weekly goals. Normal weight loss is right around 1-2 lbs. per week. If someone is trying to lose a significant amount of weight, normally that number is just a bit higher. In the same example, weekly goals would consist of completing all of the workouts and staying clean with the nutrition, along with losing 2 lbs. Again, very attainable and not daunting.

Last, focus on monthly goals. This is where I like to cut it off. I don't like going beyond monthly goals because then the goals can begin to seem like they are too much. I don't want you getting discouraged. In the example above, a good weight loss goal for one month would be 8-10 lbs. However, if you find yourself losing 4-5 lbs. per week, instead of 1-2 lbs., you can quickly adjust your monthly goal to what you feel is attainable. I want to add, though, that all of your goals, whether daily, weekly, or monthly, should be challenging. It's important that you push yourself outside of your comfort zone. If you are losing 4-5 lbs. per week instead of 1-2 lbs., don't allow yourself to settle for a monthly goal of losing just 8 lbs. Instead, set that goal at 20 lbs.

Just like with your "why," your goals have to be visible, meaning you have to write them down and put them somewhere you will see them every day. This is mainly for your weekly and monthly goals. Something I recommend you do is purchase a large dry erase board and stick it somewhere you will see it every day, such as your living room wall or office. Once again, when you can see your goals daily, you are reminded of what you need to do to keep moving toward them.

For daily goals, get yourself a daily planner — an actual paper book planner or one you use on your phone or computer. I don't care either way. This is so that you have structure and organization. Each evening before you unplug, take 10-15 minutes and create a to-do list for the next day. That to-do list becomes your daily goal list. Don't allow yourself to stop working each day until all of those tasks on that list have been completed. Remember this, daily goals lead to achieving weekly goals, which lead to achieving monthly goals and then eventually long-term goals!

STEP 9: ELIMINATING PROCRASTINATION AND TAKING ACTION

Here I am yet again talking about taking action. Is it too much? Nope. It's the most important aspect of success. Without action there are no results. You can't sit on your ass and wait for change to happen; you have to make it happen! But you have to make it happen now. Not tomorrow, not a month or year from now, now!

Procrastination has become a disease too. Let me ask you this. How many times have you thought about doing something and really wanted to do it, but put it off so long that you completely forgot about it? Probably quite a bit. It happens all the time. And yes, I'm even guilty of it from time to time. Procrastination is easy, taking action is hard. I explained that thoroughly already in the "Fear of Change" section. It's tough to take action and that's why most people don't do it. You might become extremely motivated after reading this book, but the real test is how quickly you respond to the information and apply it to your life. Once again, odds are that you won't do shit with what you learn here. You will think about doing it, but never actually do it. Eventually as time goes on, you slowly begin to forget about all of the excellent tips, and then what's in the book all together. Then you basically just wasted quite a few hours of your life. Obviously, I don't want that to happen and neither should you.

I'm going to get real with you for a moment and talk about something that nobody enjoys talking about, death. We are all going to die some day. That's reality. But still, it's almost like we've adopted the mindset that we are invincible and will live forever. We will not. Every single one of us will leave this earth at some point just as the millions before us have. We have a very small timespan here. We purposely ignore the truth because the truth sucks. A lot of people fear death. It's scary, sure. What's even scarier is not truly living life and reaching your full potential.

Do you want to know what my greatest fear is? Being 90 years old on my deathbed and regretting all the things I should have done. That scares the hell out of me! I don't want to be full of regret right before my time is up. That would be awful. But this is the reality facing a majority of people. I can't imagine that feeling, I just can't. That is why I'm doing everything I can to enjoy life, experience incredible things, take action on the things I want to and should do, and leave behind an incredible legacy.

How are you going to live your life? Take a second and think about what will be running through your mind on your deathbed. You might get a terrible feeling in your gut after realizing that, if you continue on the same path you're on, you'll become that person full of regret. Think about it long and hard. That feeling you're experiencing right now can be a huge motivator to take action now and make a change. That's what I'm hoping. But I will die, you will die, we will all die eventually. Keep putting things off and, before you know it, it will be too late.

I know a lot of incredibly smart people. I also know a lot of people who have an average IQ. I know some people who truly aren't that smart at all. But let me explain something to you. Your ability to become successful has nothing to do with how smart you are! It has everything to do with your ability to not procrastinate and take action.

I'm not a genius, not even close to it. I'm not stupid either, but I would consider myself to be someone with an average IQ. So how can I, an average person, become far more successful than someone who is much smarter than me? Because there are a hell of a lot of smart people out there who procrastinate and don't take action when they have ideas. And many of them have a ton of incredible ideas. Just because you're smart doesn't mean you're successful or going to be successful. It's interesting because there are a lot of arrogant super smart people who automatically believe that being smart will allow them to win at life. That's not the case. You get a cookie for winning with the genetic code, that's it. Whether or not you become successful depends on your ability to take action.

"Think. Act. Become." That's a phrase that my father taught me. "Act" is the essential part of the equation. You can't think something and then automatically become it. You have to act on those thoughts and ideas and then you will become. From this point forward, I want you to start acting. Take action on what you learn in this book. Take action on all the incredible ideas that you have running through your head on a daily basis. If you want to do something, do it! Stop procrastinating and take action now.

STEP 10: GAINING SELF-CONFIDENCE AND BELIEF

Next time you go shopping, take five minutes and study people around you. Yes, I want you to people watch. Sit down on a bench and watch the people walk by. Don't do it in a creepy way, of course, but watch how they walk and their body language when they communicate. It's very easy to pick out those who have self-confidence and those who don't. Self-confident people all have the same characteristics. They smile a lot, stand tall, look people in the eye, and walk briskly. Confidence just spews out of them! Others tend to gravitate toward self-confident people. You will often see these people with a bunch of friends around them. They are always laughing and having a good time. You can always tell a self-confident person from someone who lacks confidence.

Those with low self-confidence are also very easy to pick out. They slouch when they walk, don't look others in the eye, have a permanent frown, and walk slowly. Most of the time, they are alone. They have absolutely no belief in themselves and it becomes very obvious. Now that you have watched others, it's time to reflect on yourself. Which characteristics do you have? Are you in the confident or not confident category? There's a good chance you come to the realization that you possess a lot of the characteristics of a non-confident person. That's OK, we will switch that around.

Success doesn't happen without confidence. I feel I've been successful in most aspects of my life. None of that success would have been possible if I didn't have confidence in myself and my abilities. I've also met and have become great friends with a lot of successful people. None of them lacks confidence. Not a single one. Think about the successful people you know and whether or not they have confidence. I'm guessing that they are all highly confident people. You can't lead others if you're not confident in yourself. Others can't be confident in you if you aren't confident in yourself. Confidence breeds confidence.

I'm going to use my old financial advising job as an example. Let's say that you're looking for a new financial advisor to manage your money. When you meet with potential advisors, will you choose someone with a weak handshake, who hesitates when they talk, who won't look you in the eye? Or are you going to choose the advisor who comes into the meeting standing tall, with a giant smile, firm handshake, who looks you right in the eye and never hesitates about what they are talking about? Obviously, you will choose the one who's confident. Duh, right? But why? Because someone who isn't confident in themselves won't have confidence in managing your money either. You know that. You can feel it. Your money is precious. You want to make sure it's in the right hands. You will be confident in the advisor who is confident in him or herself and his or her ability to manage your money effectively.

I want you to understand something that's very important. You are only as big as your belief. Write down "I AM ONLY AS BIG AS MY BELIEF!" and repeat it to yourself over and over again until it sinks in. If you have to, put it on a post-it note and stick it on your computer or on your bathroom mirror so you can see it every day. If you believe that you are a piece of shit, well golly, you're going to be a piece of shit. If you believe you are a badass, you're going to be a badass. What you believe is what you become.

There are too many people who use negative, self-demeaning words to describe themselves daily. They look in the mirror and think "I'm fat," "I'm not good enough," "I can't do this," or

"I'm ugly." Their negative thoughts determine the person they become, and it shows in everything they do. They are the people who walk with their heads down, slouch, walk slowly, don't look others in the eye, and don't have many friends.

I want you to do this. You have to replace all those negative, self-demeaning thoughts with positive affirmations. When you catch yourself thinking that you're not good enough, immediately replace that with "I am good enough" and "I can do this!" You are good enough. I promise you are. You will become what you think. Try this exercise, too. Next time you are out and about, I want you to be conscious of your body language. Force yourself to smile, stand tall, walk a little faster, look people in the eye and tell them "hello." Maybe even walk with a little swagger. You're not going to believe how much better you feel when you act confident. Even if you're faking it for now, that's OK. Do it long enough and it will become your reality. Walk around thinking to yourself "I'm a badass" and everything will begin to change. You will become that badass! Try it.

The majority of people sell themselves short because they don't believe they can achieve anything. They don't understand that they can actually accomplish anything they set their minds to. They might want to get into shape, but don't believe they can commit to it. They might want to make a career change, but don't believe they can make the change. They might want a promotion at work, but don't believe in themselves enough to go ask for one. They might want to start up a side job, but don't believe they could make it work. I could go on and on. You are doomed from the start with this mentality. But one small shift in mindset can make the difference between someone who barely makes ends meet and someone with total financial and time freedom. It really does all come down to your belief. You can't even make it out of the gate without belief! Rather, you'll be that horse that stands still and watches all the other horses take off and leave you behind. That's life. Those with belief in themselves sprint out of the gate, while those who don't remain stagnant in a lifestyle they don't particularly enjoy. When you have belief, the rest follows, but it all starts with belief.

How do you think I landed my wife? She's smoking hot. It's because I was confident in myself the day we met, and she found that extremely attractive. But I have total belief in my ability to be a great father, husband, friend, businessman, and mentor and that's the only reason I have become successful in all of those areas. It's time for you to have belief in yourself and your capabilities as well. Once you do, watch out world, you're going to become a freight train that can't be stopped!

Changing Your Health

Now it's time to really dig in to how to become healthy. When I first started writing the book, I named this section "how to get fitness results," but then I quickly realized that fitness is just one aspect of being healthy. I want to teach you everything I know about truly becoming healthy, not just becoming fit. There is a difference. Looking fit means nothing if you aren't healthy.

Since becoming a fitness coach, and especially since dealing with a chronic disease, I have spent countless hours researching nutrition, supplementation, and workouts. I have this drive within me to learn as much as I possibly can regarding health and fitness. Am I a doctor? No. Am I certified in nutrition? No. Am I a certified personal trainer? No. I don't feel a certification makes me any more or less knowledgeable. It's just not necessary in my opinion.

I've gained an incredible amount of knowledge through personal experience and research. I'm pretty sure I have more knowledge than most who are certified anyway. All I know is this. I've had an incredible transformation. I've done years of research. And when I was battling Lyme and got bloodwork done, I was deficient in just about every vitamin, had liver and kidney issues, my triglycerides were all out of whack, among many other issues. After gaining an incredible amount of knowledge about nutrition, detoxing, and herbs and had my bloodwork redone, my naturopath was in shock with just how perfect my numbers came back. That all happened because of the changes I made (not what any doctor recommended) over the course of two years. I do know my stuff when it comes to improving health.

One thing I want to remind you as you're going through these next couple of chapters, though, is that If you decide to follow any of my advice you are doing so at your own risk. It's always best to check with your doctor before making any changes.

Before I get started I have a question to ask you. Do you feel that getting healthy is complex? You said "yes" didn't you? It's not complex, I promise. It seems that way because of all the fad diets and millions of workouts available. The hardest part of it all are the mindset changes you have to make. When you can make those changes everything else seems to follow rather smoothly and easily. But becoming healthy and achieving results is quite simple. It comes down to just three important steps. The first is detoxing the body; the second is changing your nutrition; and the third is exercising consistently.

STEP 1: DETOXING THE BODY

Most people live in a toxic state. You can blame that on the air we breathe, food we consume, what we drink, what we put on our bodies, what we touch, and even what we use to clean our houses. Chemicals, toxins, and pesticides are rampant in this wonderful world of ours. Most food and products you find in stores aren't natural and are tearing down immune systems day by day.

Too many people trust advertisements and blindly purchase products without understanding what it is they are actually buying, with no regard to how these products affect their health. When you wake up to the fact that most companies don't give a shit about your health and only care about profits, you start paying attention to everything you use and consume. Too many people put their trust in the government and various companies, believing that they always have the right intentions and are looking out for your health. That is unfortunately not always the case. In fact, most of the time it's not the case. They just don't care.

Shortly after I was diagnosed with Lyme Disease, I finally began to understand this and started looking into everything I used and consumed. It's an important habit to acquire. I had an "awakening" and I'm hoping that reading this helps you have one too. I don't care what company it is, flip the product over and look into the ingredients list. That means you might have to do a little research until you gain the knowledge necessary to under-stand ingredients that can be potentially detrimental to your health. Thank goodness we have smartphones now, allowing us to quickly research anything, even right there in the store. If you don't know what something is, Google it and understand it. You can't go wrong doing this. Will it take a few extra minutes? Sure, but those few extra minutes can have a drastic effect on your health. And as you become familiar with certain ingredients, over time you will have to do less and less research.

When our bodies are in a toxic state, we are much more suscep-tible to cancer, diseases, and other health issues. It is estimated that 1,735,350 new cases of cancer will be diagnosed in the U.S. in 2018[1]. That's a lot. Maybe you're reading this after 2018 and that number turned out to be greater. Regardless, it's apparent there is a serious problem. With Lyme Disease, there will be

---

1   https://www.cancer.gov/about-cancer/understanding/statistics

about 300,000 new cases diagnosed each year[2]. What's interesting about that stat, though, is the amount of undiagnosed cases. Lyme mimics so many other diseases that statistic probably is drastically higher. What's crazy is that that's just one disease among thousands diagnosed. Disease and cancer are common. They shouldn't be, but they are because of how weak we have made our immune systems.

Our immune systems can't function properly when the body is overrun with toxins. I'm sure this was the case with me back in 2015 and why I developed a chronic illness. Years of poor eating habits and the lack of detoxing led to a severely weakened immune system. If I would have made proper choices early on, more than likely I would have never developed this disease. But hindsight is 20/20, right? Unfortunately, it is.

Most people go through life with poor health habits, never worrying about cancer, disease, or other illnesses until it's too late. The old cliché "you don't know what you have until it's gone" is more true than you can imagine when it comes to your health. There is not much worse than having your health ripped away from you. Trust me, I know. As soon as it happens, you instantly regret all the decisions you made up to that point. I know I did. When the ability to do the things you normally do and feel the way you normally feel suddenly gets stripped from you, you quickly realize just how important good health really is. I will never take my health for granted again as long as I live. I recommend that you do the same. Your health is everything.

But to succeed in this, you have to actually pause and think about your actions and what they are doing to your health. You have to get out of the habit of acting on impulse. You can't even begin

---

2   http://www.ilads.org/lyme/lyme-quickfacts.php

to move in the right direction if you are functioning in a toxic state. The first step is to detox your body and what you surround yourselves with. You have to go through a "detox your life" phase.

Before I go on, I want you to understand something, though. This is difficult. Many of the products you normally use will have to be thrown out or donated. That's just the reality if you are truly trying to improve your health. I get that it's tough to make such massive changes overnight and I'm not asking you to do so. Some of these things you can do immediately, others are going to take some time. Just remember, it's a process. Start off by doing a few things here and there.

Sweating

One of the major ways that we can detox the skin is by sweating, and the best routes to a detoxifying sweat comes with exercise and using a sauna. When I was going through the heart of my Lyme treatment, I learned that I had to constantly flush out all of the dead bacteria that were sitting stagnant in my body after I killed them off with treatment. If I didn't detox regularly, I would have found myself becoming even sicker.

I wasn't able to exercise because of low energy and flu-like symptoms daily, so a sauna became the best option. After much research, I decided upon an infrared sauna because it penetrates the skin and detoxes the body on a cellular level[3]. Traditional saunas just heat the outside of the body. Infrared saunas are excellent in helping you detox from heavy metals and other fat-soluble toxins. They are also great for chronic pain management and reduction, improved circulation, and relaxation. It definitely helped quite a bit with my pain.

---

3   https://draxe.com/infrared-sauna/

When I was going through the bulk of my Lyme treatment, I used the sauna three to four times a week for about 40 minutes each session. You don't want to go much longer than that, though, for the risk of overheating and becoming dehydrated. After getting out of the sauna, it's important to rehydrate by drinking high-quality water. You don't have to buy an expensive sauna, for affordable infrared saunas are available. If you don't want to buy one, some gyms contain regular and infrared saunas. But every time you consume alcohol, use products with chemicals, eat foods that aren't natural, you are putting toxins right into your body and a sauna can help you detox. It's something that I highly recommend using at least once every week or two, sometimes more depending on your health situation.

After I finished all of my Lyme treatment and started working out intensely again, some of my symptoms began to reappear. I was sure that I had pretty much gotten rid of the majority of the Lyme bacteria, so this confused me. I figured this resulted from release of toxins I still had deep within my muscle cells. Now here's the thing. I don't know if what I just stated is actually a fact. There is a lot of conflicting information about the role of exercising in detoxing. All I can do is share my own personal experience when it comes to this.

The lifting, jumping, and intense cardio improved my circulation, therefore helping me move around and flush out toxins sitting stagnant in my body. When I lifted heavy, I felt sick again, and this happened for a few months. However, the more I did it, the less severe the symptoms became. Over time, all the symptoms disappeared.

If I could have somehow forced myself to work out while I was going through treatment, even if it was short and not too intense, I think I could have sped up my recovery. So, if you ask me, I believe intense exercise, specifically resistance training, plays some sort of role in cleansing toxins deep within the body and muscle cells. What is proven, though, is that sweating detoxes the skin, so if you're working out regularly and sweating while doing so, you are detoxing. Exercising daily is important anyways, this is just another reason to do so.

Epsom salt baths

In my detox research, I kept coming across all the benefits of an Epsom salt bath. Now listen, I'm not the kind of guy to take baths. For one, sitting in the same spot for a period of time and you know that's tough for me. Two, it's a bath and, come on, most men don't take baths. But I swallowed my pride, bought some Epsom salts, put a scoop of those bad boys in a running bath, and sat my ass in it multiple times throughout my detoxing journey. Hell, even to this day, I still take Epsom salt baths when I feel I need to detox.

Epsom salt baths are great because they remove toxins from the body and put magnesium and sulfate back in. Many people are deficient in magnesium because of poor nutrition. I was extremely deficient while battling the disease. Magnesium plays an important role in removing toxins, muscle control, and energy production[4], and the sulfates aid in detoxification. Normally, I add 2 cups of Epsom salts and soak for 30-40 minutes. Some Epsom salts have essential oils added, such as lavender, not just for smell, but for other health benefits as well. I have to caution you, though, don't just go out and purchase any Epsom salts. Do your research. There are a lot of brands that add chemicals. Obviously, you don't want that if your focus is on detoxing.

---

4   https://draxe.com/magnesium-supplements/

Green tea with lemon

Every morning during my Lyme treatment I drank on an empty stomach hot green tea with a lemon squeezed into it. I did this to leverage the powerful detoxing effects and other benefits of green tea, which contains polyphenols, which aid the body's detox system. It's also been shown to help prevent some heart-related problems, such as high blood pressure and heart failure[5]. Lemon juice aids the liver in flushing out toxins and contains a ton of Vitamin C (antioxidant), which counteracts free radical damage.

Water purification

Most people don't think twice about heading into the kitchen, flipping on that faucet, and drinking the water straight from the tap. Maybe you're even someone who used to chug from the hose growing up. I used to. However, the older I've gotten and the more wisdom I've gained in the area of health and nutrition, I've concluded that probably wasn't the best thing to do. Did it kill me? Nah. I'm still here. But unfortunately, most tap water today contains a ridiculous amount of toxins, such as chlorine, fluoride, mercury, arsenic, PCBs, dioxins, other heavy metals, and even pesticides and antibiotics.[6] There's a lot more I left off the list, but you get the point.

Consuming toxic substances on a daily basis over a long period of time can weaken the immune system and trigger a lot of health issues. It's just like stuffing your face full of fast food every day. It might not affect you the next day, but over time it will most certainly lead to some problems. Maybe you're sitting there mumbling something about the EPA and how they make

---

5   https://www.webmd.com/food-recipes/features/health-benefits-of-green-tea#1

6   https://www.globalhealingcenter.com/natural-health/12-toxins-in-your-drinking-water/

sure all water that we consume is safe. If I could insert a blank stare emoji here I would, because I trust the EPA about as much as I trust a fart after eating Taco Bell. They just set limits for contaminants so the water doesn't get "too toxic." Water is the most important thing for our bodies, so it's important to make sure the water we drink is pure!

Bottled water is a better option, but really isn't as good as you think — and it's expensive. Most people think they buy some kind of purity when they purchase bottled water, but most bottled water is just moderately filtered tap water. So, what can you do?

There are a few different options. I went the route of purchasing a high-quality reverse osmosis (RO) filtering system to place under my kitchen sink. It ran me about $400 and was easy to install myself. Most RO systems remove 99% of all toxins found in normal tap water, but many also remove a lot of the minerals. The system I got actually adds minerals back in during one of the stages of filtering. Be aware, though, that most RO systems also make the water slightly acidic, but you can find some that can make it slightly alkaline. It's important to keep the body slightly alkaline. An acidic body PH can lead to disease and the development of cancer. Later in the book I will talk about foods that will help you keep the body out of an acidic state.

The other option is distilled water. Again, one of the problems with this is that everything is stripped from the water, including the minerals, and it can get expensive. If you go this route, make sure that you add a pinch of Himalayan Salt to your water every time you get a glass. Himalayan Salt is loaded with healthy minerals.

We also have installed a whole house filtration system, which cost about $400 and needed to be professionally installed. With installation, it set us back right around $1,500, but the cost was well worth it. It's one of the best decisions we've made. The whole house system helps purify the water throughout the entire house. Obviously. Now you might be asking, "Why would I do that?" Did you know that your skin absorbs pretty much everything that it comes in contact with? So, when you take a shower, not only are all the toxins in the water absorbed by the body, but you're also breathing them in through the steam. Not good if you have crap water quality. The same with washing your hands. Swimming pools, sprinkler systems, same thing. If getting a whole house filter isn't possible, consider something as simple as a shower head filter. In the end, there are many steps you can take to improve the quality of water in your home.

Body products

Most people purchase certain deodorant or antiperspirants because the commercials are badass. I'm not going to lie, they are badass and enjoyable to watch, but that doesn't mean the products are healthy. It just means that the companies have a good understanding of their markets and how to appeal to them effectively. These companies could care less about how their product affects your health. Don't worry, I fell into the trap too. Before I made the shift, I would buy based on marketing, smell, and effectiveness. Now, though, I purchase based on effectiveness and quality ingredients. Marketing of a product doesn't mean anything to me anymore and it shouldn't to you either. I see right past the bullshit and pay attention to what's actually important. From this point on, you should take the same approach and start being conscious about what exactly is being marketed to you.

Let me dig into antiperspirants for just a minute for you skeptics out there. One of the main ingredients in many antiperspirants is aluminum, which clogs the pores and causes you to not sweat, at least not as much. You sweat for a reason! I already explained that. You need to sweat to get rid of toxins. If you can't sweat, those toxins build up. To make matters worse, most antiperspirants (and deodorants) contain other chemicals and toxins, such as parabens, phthalates, and fragrance, which all can lead to specific issues on their own.[7] Have no fear, your local organic grocery store stocks some great options for deodorant and antiperspirant. Just a quick Google search will help as well.

Shampoo, hand soap, toothpaste, cosmetics, lotions, shaving cream all follow along the same lines. Most are crap and millions of people reach for these products daily without thinking twice. Think about this for a second. Every time you use shampoo, put on deodorant, wash your hands, put on lotion, use shaving cream, or put on makeup, you add toxins into your body. If you're not detoxing regularly to eliminate those toxins, you become a ticking time bomb for health problems, sometimes serious ones. Once again, toxic overload destroys your immune system, allowing diseases and cancer to thrive. Listen, all I'm asking you to do is a little research. Stop trusting these brands and playing ignorant to the fact that the products you're using daily are doing more harm than good. Look into everything you purchase and understand exactly what you're putting on your body.

Home products

Just like with the products you put on your body, nobody takes much time to think about other products they use around the house, such as cleaning wipes, cleaners, sprays, detergents, candles, and dishwasher fluids. There are just as many, if not more toxins in these products. Every time you use a cleaning wipe, for example, toxins are absorbed into your hands. And how many times have you wiped off the counter and then put your

---

7   http://time.com/4394051/deodorant-antiperspirant-toxic/

food (such as vegetables) on the counter to cut up? I'm imagining quite a bit. Those chemicals that you just wiped onto your counter are now on your food.

And when you use dishwashing fluid, there's always residue left over on the dishes that is absorbed by the body by touching the dishes or ingested. So, every time you put food on that plate and start eating, every bite contains just a little bit of chemicals. Yum. Nothing like some chicken with perfume and bleach. Wait, what? Yeah, I decided to check out the ingredients real quick in one of the major dishwasher detergents. Perfume and bleach were just two of many toxic chemicals listed. It's small things like this that nobody takes the time to think about, but can have a drastic effect on our health if consumed over a period of time.

Let's talk about those lovely, great-smelling candles the ladies love lighting up all over the house. You walk in the house, close your eyes, take a deep breath in through your nose and experience the amazing aroma of a candle named "Grandma's Apple Pie." Man, that's some good stuff! But here's the buzzkill. Most of the candles anymore are made of paraffin wax, which gives off carcinogenic fumes when burned. Not only do you get fragrance (a chemical shit storm) from the scented ones, but chemicals like benzene and toluene are common and released into the air, which of course you then breathe in.

According to the World Health Organization, benzene is a "well-established cause of cancer in humans."[8] And according to the U.S. Department of Labor, "Toluene affects the central nervous system, eyes, skin, respiratory system, liver, and kidneys. Breathing high levels of toluene during pregnancy has been shown to result in children with birth defects and to hinder

---

8   http://www.who.int/ipcs/features/benzene.pdf

mental abilities and growth."[9] But yet, these carcinogens are being added to candles that are purchased daily all around the world. Now do you believe me when I say that most companies don't have your health in mind when creating and selling products? Always research. And seriously, stop buying candles that contain paraffin wax!

Sorry if I just juiced your anxiety, but you need to know these things. I told you my eyes have been opened after being diagnosed with Lyme disease and I wasn't kidding. I was clueless about all of this stuff before! I blindly went through life never thinking about how the products I used affected my health. But Melinda and I have made some incredible changes that I believe will positively impact not just our health, but our kids' health as well. Again, there are so many incredible, natural, and organic brands out there for home and body products. You just have to do a little research. Will it cost a little extra? Probably, but again, you either pay for it now or pay for it later with poor health and medication. Please start being conscious of the products you use!

You can get a PDF of all of my favorite high-quality home and body products at www.JoshSpencer.com/book

Parasite cleanses

There's a good chance you're reading this with some sort of parasite just chilling in your intestines. Nasty, I know, but it's common. A number of different parasites can live inside you and have drastic effects on your immune system and the absorption of nutrients. Most of the time, we get them through poorly cooked meat, such as pork and chicken. However, we can also get them from fecal matter from others who have been infected, and from bugs as well. Wait, what? Believe it or not, a lot of studies have

---

9   https://www.osha.gov/SLTC/toluene/health_hazards.html

shown that most of the things we touch and some of the things we eat have human shit on them.

Here's a great example. Have you ever been to a bar? Sure you have. Let's say Jimmy the bartender decides to head to the bathroom to take a squirt. He then washes his hands, which he should do, but then turns the faucet off with his hands instead of using a paper towel. Little did he know that Mick was in there 20 minutes ago and absolutely destroyed the toilet after chowing down on a burrito. When wiping, Mick got just a little bit on his hands. It doesn't take much. When he went to wash his hands, he turned on the faucet with the hand that had a little extra microscopic sauce on it. Since Jimmy just shut the faucet off, he too now has a little extra sauce on his hands. Jimmy comes out and there you are ready for a drink. You order a rum and diet with a *GULP* lime. Jimmy grabs the lime, squeezes it into your drink, and there you go, you now have a parasitic rum and diet. Sorry if I just made you yak, but things like this happen! This is why it's important to occasionally go through some sort of parasite cleanse. You can take some precautions of course, but most of the time it's out of your control.

I thought this would be a fitting moment to share my process after I go to the bathroom. I'm a germ freak, so sharing this process with you brings me joy. My wife and kids know this process as well. You're welcome.

Step 1 - Get paper towel.

Step 2 - Turn on sink with paper towel.

Step 3 - Wash hands thoroughly with soap.

Step 4 - Turn off sink with paper towel (make sure you're grabbing the clean side).

Step 5 - Use same paper towel to get another paper towel.

Step 6 - Dry hands with new paper towel.

Step 7 - Open door with new paper towel and throw it away in the basket.

When choosing a parasite cleanse, try to go the natural route. Most of the natural cleanses use herbs like cloves, wormwood, and black walnut, but a few other herbs and a product called diatomaceous earth are very effective as well. Do your research and talk to your doctor to find the best for you. And seriously, start using a paper towel to shut off the water and open up the door in the bathroom! Carrying around a bottle of hand sanitizer isn't a bad idea either. Just make sure it doesn't contain added chemicals.

Apple cider vinegar

I like to take a shot when I wake up in the morning. No, not that kind of shot, that was back in college. I'm talking about a shot of apple cider vinegar! Every morning, I have a shot of Bragg's Organic Apple Cider Vinegar, mixing one tablespoon with a ¼ cup of water and chugging it on an empty stomach. I even started doing the same at night. Studies have shown that doing so right before bed helps lower blood sugar levels.[10] It also plays a role in liver detoxification and boosts energy as well.[11]

---

10   https://articles.mercola.com/apple-cider-vinegar-benefits-uses.aspx
11   https://articles.mercola.com/apple-cider-vinegar-benefits-uses.aspx

Cayenne pepper

This spicy pepper has incredible detoxifying effects, all thanks to a natural compound it contains called capsaicin. This helps with blood pressure and circulation, aiding in removing wastes from the blood. It also helps reduce pain.[12] You can add cayenne pepper to your food or drink. An excellent detox drink is to add lemon and cayenne pepper to water. I don't use cayenne often, but I started using it more on my food after learning all the benefits.

Colonics & enemas

This is the second time I have to bring up the topic of shit and I swear this is the last time I'll talk about it in the book. When you're talking about detoxing, I guess it's bound to be discussed. Regardless, an enema or colonics treatment deliver multiple detoxing benefits. I came across both of these multiple times in my research while dealing with Lyme Disease. However, after learning about what exactly they were, I had no desire to actually do them until one of my natural doctors repeatedly brought it up to me. Eventually and reluctantly, I scheduled an appointment to have it done.

Constantly consuming and absorbing toxins affects the digestive system and the colon can become backed up because of the toxins, causing various health issues. During a colonics treatment, a tube inserted into the rectum shoots up clean, warm water into the colon. The water builds up in the colon and then is expelled, along with feces and toxins. The whole process normally takes an hour.

I went through multiple colonics treatments while battling Lyme Disease and there's no denying it's awful and uncomfortable. The

---

12   https://articles.mercola.com/vitamins-supplements/capsaicin.aspx

worst part is when the nurse has to come in and make sure you inserted the tube correctly. You sit there with your legs and ass up just doing your best not to make eye contact. I just stared at the ceiling thinking about anything other than what was actually happening. I felt completely violated. Will I do it again? Nope. Five times was plenty.

As funny as the story is, though, and no matter how awkward it was, just like everything else I did, it helped me detox and prepare my body to fight the disease on its own. I was willing to go to whatever lengths necessary to get my health back. There are an incredible amount of health benefits from a colonics treatment. If you're battling your own health issues, it might be something worth considering.

Enemas are the little brother of colonics treatments. You can do enemas at home if you want privacy. You use a little bag and tube to insert various fluids into the rectum, wait a certain amount of time, and then expel the fluid along with feces. It cleanses the colon just like a colonics treatment. OK that's it, I'm done talking about it. Ugh.

Massages

Ever since I was financially capable of doing so, I've done my best to get massages at least once every few weeks because of the many health benefits. Not only does it help with muscle recovery, it helps with detoxification as well. When you get a massage, the gentle squeezing and stroking of the muscles helps draw out toxins from in between the muscles and cells. The toxins enter the circulatory system to be flushed from the body.

The lymph system works with the circulatory system to get rid of bacteria and viruses. A toxic overload in the lymph system makes it sluggish, and immune cells can't properly be transported around the body to fight infections. Massages can help move around and eliminate those toxins so that the lymph and circulatory systems can do their jobs.

Massages, specifically lymphatic drainage massages, can be very helpful with detoxification. It was very beneficial for me when I was going through the heart of my Lyme treatment. They are also great for stress relief. Stress suppresses the immune system. You might have noticed that when you're stressed, you tend to get sick or experience cold sores. It's because the immune system has a tough time suppressing viruses and a regular massage can help relax you. So yes, make an appointment to get a massage. Your body will thank you. Try to get a massage at least once every few weeks.

Other methods

There are a lot of other methods of detoxing that are very effective. One that I have done multiple times that has worked well for me is a 21-day gentle cleanse that involves using certain natural supplements and temporarily shifting to an all vegan diet high in fruits and vegetables. I just want to make it clear that I'm not vegan. I have nothing against the vegan lifestyle, but it's not for me. I will just do a vegan cleanse once every year or so to help detox my body.

Another method is juicing. Basically, juicing is the process of extracting juice from fruits and vegetables. As I was searching for detoxing methods with Lyme, I kept coming across juicing, but never got around to actually trying it. But there are lots of benefits if you do it the right way. I encourage you to do your own research and talk to your doctor about finding the right detoxing method.

STEP 2: CHANGING YOUR NUTRITION

My nutrition was terrible growing up. I didn't eat healthy. I used to think that fried chicken fingers were healthy because it was chicken. Maybe that's you now. I just didn't know better. And no, by the way, fried chicken fingers are not healthy. Most fried foods are loaded with trans fats, which aren't good for you. Many foods are fried using vegetable oil. Funny how it's called vegetable oil, almost making you believe it's good for you, but it's not. In fact, it's terrible. Vegetable oils, such as corn oil, soybean oil, canola oil, safflower, and sunflower oils, are high in Omega-6, which are highly inflammatory.

I had very serious unexplained illnesses come and go several times a year. I believe it had everything to do with my poor nutrition. In addition, my poor eating habits played the biggest role in why I could never achieve my fitness goals in college. Only when I started making major changes to my nutrition did I start to achieve my goals and reduce the amount of times I got sick. In fact, I went years and years without getting sick. Lyme was really the first major sickness that I experienced for about five years. I didn't even get a simple cold in that time.

Proper nutrition leverages everything. If you want to gain mass, you have to eat right. If you want to lean out, you have to eat right. If you want to truly become healthy, you have to eat right. There's just no going around it. It drives me nuts when clients persist in not changing their diet. They believe they can get results by just working out. That's true to a point. They might get stronger and maybe lose a little body fat, but they will quickly hit a plateau. Nutrition is key. Not working out, nutrition. Working out is just a part of it.

Remember, I'm trying to teach you how to become healthy, not just look good. There's a difference. If you want to be healthy, you must eat healthy. You're going to have to make some changes in what you're eating. Accept it. Embrace it. I don't expect you to make all of these changes immediately, though. This is going to be a process just like everything else, but the quicker you can make these changes the better. If you're the type who can go from eating terrible to following a set plan 100% right away, by all means go for it. That's how I am. But if you need to slowly integrate this new lifestyle, that's OK too. In the next few sections I'm going to go into great detail about the steps you can take, what foods to eat, and what to watch out for.

Cleaning out the cupboards

You can't eat what's not there. That was a big thing for me when I started that home workout program in 2008. I had a problem where I would snack on whatever I could get my hands on when I was hungry. Most people snack on high-carb foods. I did. Maybe you do too. But one of the very first things I did when I decided to fully commit to a new lifestyle was go through all of my cupboards and either throw away or donate anything that didn't fit my plan. Cookies, ice cream, cereal, all gone. Then, whenever I had those cravings or needed a snack, I had to choose a healthier alternative. I highly suggest that you do the same if you're trying to make changes to your health.

Shifting to organic

It always irritates me when people get defensive and say, "Well I can't afford organic food." It's narrow-minded. You already know how I feel about the "I can't afford it" excuse. However, I'm not expecting you to go organic right away. If you can, great. If not, that's OK too. It's a process, but organic is the best way to go. If you are truly looking to change your health, you have to ulti-mately adopt an organic lifestyle. If not, you're still putting too many toxins into your body and risking serious health issues. Once again, I understand first-hand just how tough it can be to go from having terrible eating habits to consuming solely organic food. Melinda and I didn't do it right away. It took us time. We started eating healthier, switching to more fruits, veggies, lean meats and whole grains, but not 100% organic initially. Once I learned that even those "healthy" products contained pesticides and other unnatural chemicals and toxins, we shifted to buying just organic.

Sure, it is a tiny bit more expensive, but the difference between organic and non-organic is pretty big for your health. Remember, if you don't pay for it now you will pay for it later in some way, maybe even by battling cancer or a serious disease. Hopefully that's not the case, of course, but constantly consuming toxins can eventually lead you there. Your body needs to be in as much of a non-toxic state as possible if you want to maintain good health. Plus, once you make the shift to organic food, you will taste a difference. In my opinion, organic food tastes much better and I'm sure you will think so too. That's what our bodies want! I challenge you to just try it out and see what you think.

Food suppliers have gotten smart. The majority remain uneth-ical assholes, but as much as I hate to admit it, they are smart business people. They have noticed the increasing trend of eating healthier and have adjusted their marketing strategies accord-ingly. That's the reason you see a lot of "fat free," "sugar free," "natural," and "multigrain" products on the shelves. They also might use phrases like "supports healthy joints" or "made with whole grains." They have even gone as far as purposely naming the product something that sounds healthy.

I'm here to caution you, though: Just because you see those words on labels doesn't mean it's good for you. Usually a "fat free" product is loaded with sugar. If it's "sugar free," it's loaded with artificial sweeteners (that means chemicals). The term "natural" is deceiving. In the past, "natural" wasn't regulated at all. After many people complained, the FDA gave it a definition — nothing artificial can be added to the food product. But hold on a minute. "Natural" products can still contain pesticides, hormones, and other chemicals. Apparently, those are natural? Not in my definition. Ignore the "natural" label when you come across it.

What about "multigrain?" Suppliers created the term "multigrain" to sound similar to a term that most people associate with healthy, "whole grain." Go down any bread aisle and you will see a ton of "multigrain" products. Multigrain might contain whole grain, but not entirely. It can be jam packed with sugar, enriched white flour, and other crap. The examples I used are just a few of the many terms created to trick you to think something is healthy when it's not. In the end, just keep in mind that suppliers and stores will do anything they can to sell their products, even if it means purposely deceiving consumers. Most are concerned about just one thing, profits.

Organic food is a much better route to go. If something is labeled as "organic," normally the product contains just organic ingredients. Notice I said "normally." It's not always the case. Regulations for organic products are rather complex. They are pretty strong when it comes to products grown in the U.S. but become a little questionable when the products are imported. The government relies on third-party regulators in foreign countries and they could possibly lie about whether or not it's fully organic.[13]

---

13   https://www.washingtonpost.com/news/monkey-cage/wp/2017/05/22/
       why-its-so-hard-to-know-whether-organic-food-is-really-organic/?noredi-
       rect=on&utm_term=.125f55f57a52

In addition, just because something is organic doesn't automatically make it good for you to eat. The ingredients are purer and you're not going to find dyes, pesticides, antibiotics, and other toxins, but it could be loaded with other ingredients you shouldn't be consuming in large amounts, such as sugar. For example, you can find organic cookies in most organic grocery stores. If you stuff your face full of organic cookies every day, I can assure you it's not going to help you move toward your health goals. You could have an organic cookie as a healthier snack, of course, but you shouldn't be eating them all day every day. Remember, sugar, whether it's natural or artificial, is a big reason why so many people are battling health issues.

I highly recommend that you start shopping at your local organic grocery store. Chances are you have one somewhat close to you, but if you don't, most regular grocery stores are getting more and more organic products in stock. Maybe you're still rather skeptical about buying organic food. That's OK. Let me dig a little deeper. Skepticism is fine, but it's important that you know exactly how non-organic food affects your body.

Let's begin with food dyes, which are added to many foods to make them look more appealing. The more vibrant, the more it grabs the attention of the consumer. But these dyes negatively affect our health. Let's take a product that contains Red #40, for example. Red #40 is an artificial food coloring that you might find in products like gummy bears, cereal, yogurt, and sports drinks. Most red candies contain Red#40. Studies have shown that Red #40 is a carcinogen[14] . Another common food dye, Blue #2, is linked to hyperactivity in children and cancer in mice.[15] Note what I said there. It causes hyperactivity in children. I'm saddened by how many parents blame "ADD" for their kids'

---

14   https://www.ncbi.nlm.nih.gov/pmc/articles/PMC2957945/
15   https://www.ncbi.nlm.nih.gov/pmc/articles/PMC2957945/

hyperactivity, but completely neglect the fact that poor nutrition is likely is the cause. But instead of making adjustments to nutrition, a fairly easy remedy, they put their kids on drugs that can have serious side effects. You want to avoid artificial dyes at all cost!

I have to veer off for a moment here to dig a little bit more into how people neglect the root cause of problems and go straight to pharmaceuticals to mask symptoms. This has become the mainstream way of treating people. Just because you take something and feel better doesn't mean your problem has disappeared. It's still there. Have high cholesterol? They'll just put you on statins. The majority of the time, cholesterol can be lowered naturally with proper diet and exercise. But drug companies make no money that way. Statins will be required as long as the patient continues with those poor nutrition and exercise decisions, leaving them lifelong customers of that specific drug. That's exactly what these pharmaceutical companies want.

Medications, such as statins or ADD drugs, have side effects that include muscle pain, digestive problems, liver damage, diabetes, and some other neurological side effects.[16] Many times, you will even see "death" as a possible side effect! Often, doctors need to prescribe additional drugs to deal with the additional symptoms caused by the initial medication. Now you can see why so many people take so many medications! One leads to the next and so on and so forth. It's not abnormal for people to spend thousands each month on pharmaceuticals!

The pharmaceutical industry is well over a trillion-dollar industry. Let that sink in for a moment! Medicine is a business. People are consumers. Every time we purchase a pharmaceutical we

---

16   https://www.mayoclinic.org/diseases-conditions/high-blood-cholesterol/in-depth/statin-side-effects/art-20046013

put money in their pockets, and the industry has political and financial ties just about everywhere, including with doctors. If we took a step back and started really getting to the root cause of all of these health issues instead of masking the symptoms, there wouldn't be as much of a need for pharmaceuticals. That would lead to less profits. Think that would ever happen?

Nope. The pharmaceutical industry is too powerful and corrupt. If you don't believe me, just do your research, or watch TV. Pay attention to how many pharmaceutical ads you see during an hour-long TV show. Most of the ads will be pharmaceutical ads. Pharmaceutical companies spend billions of dollars on direct advertising. But think about this for a moment. Even if a TV station wanted to stop all these ads, they couldn't. They make money through ads and removing pharmaceutical ads would significantly hurt their bottom line. These Big Pharm companies have massive power and control.

I truly feel bad for the natural doctors because they are increasingly coming under attack. It makes total sense why. By treating people naturally, such as through food and herbs, they won't be recommending pharmaceuticals, which natural doctors see as a last resort for treatment. They want to dig deep and discover the root cause, such as poor nutrition, compromised gut health, or even genetics, before prescribing pharmaceuticals. That's how it should be! Modern medicine has come a long way and it's necessary in some situations, but we don't use it properly. Now we use it to bury the truth about what is actually happening with our bodies.

Sorry about going off on that tangent. It's something that has to be addressed, though. Hopefully, from this point on, you do your best to discover the root cause of your symptoms instead of hopping on the first medication that's "recommended" for you.

Be sure to also find yourself a doctor with the same philosophy. Many times, a person can heal by shifting to an organic nutrition plan, detoxing, and establishing a healthy gut flora.

A bit ago I mentioned pesticides. Now I want to dig a little deeper. The majority of non-organic food that is available, especially fruits and vegetables, have been treated with pesticides. Why are they so commonly used? It has everything to do with money. Big food corporations want the biggest bang for their buck. Pesticides allow growers to harvest a bigger output of sellable crops. For example, maybe a grower can turn around and sell 50% of their crops without using pesticides. Without pesticides, bugs will ruin some of the crop. With pesticides, though, they might be able to sell 90%. I made up those numbers, but you get the point.

This all comes at the expense of the consumer's health. Continuous exposure to pesticides increases the risk of chronic disease, tumors, cancer, blood disorders, and nerve disorders.[17] And pesticides are literally everywhere anymore, from the food we eat to the insect sprays we use. I personally believe this is a big reason why cancer and disease has spun out of control. When you shop organic and make those changes I mentioned earlier in your home, you greatly reduce individual exposure to pesticides. Will it eliminate all the pesticides? No. You will be exposed to pesticides throughout your life. It's a big reason why detoxing regularly is important.

You might be thinking, "Well can't I just wash off my food if it's non-organic?" I wish it were that easy, but it's not. Pesticides get absorbed into the crops themselves through the roots, so no amount of washing is going to help. This is yet another reason why you should shift to an all organic diet. It's not worth the risk.

---

17   https://extension.psu.edu/potential-health-effects-of-pesticides

Last, I want to address the effects that hormones added to meat can have on us humans. For this, I really had to dig in my research, but I discovered some very startling facts. By the way, much of the non-organic meat that we eat today contains hormones. A long-term study was done on mice and rats that were given the typical hormones added to beef and chicken. Results showed increased incidences of tumors found in mammary and pituitary glands, along with the kidneys[18]. These hormones, therefore, have carcinogenic effects. Most people consume these hormones daily, sometimes multiple times daily. It's naïve to believe that this isn't having some sort of negative effect on our health and that it's not part of the reason for the increase in cancers. It's crucial for your health to make sure your meat is organic and, therefore, hormone free.

Restoring gut health

Our immune systems stem from the gut. We are not healthy if our gut is not healthy. Unfortunately, most people have poor gut health because of the overuse of antibiotics and poor nutrition. When I did my research into healing from disease, every single resource I came across talked about the importance of proper gut health for healing. I took it as a sign that maybe I, too, should focus on healing the gut.

There are billions and billions of bacteria in our gut called flora. Don't be alarmed, though, they are good bacteria and help our immune systems function normally. However, those good bacteria get wiped out by what we consume. Antibiotics cause poor gut health because they not only wipe out the bad bacteria, they wipe out the good as well. And they are incredibly overprescribed. It seems like doctors give out antibiotics like candy!

---

18   https://www.ncbi.nlm.nih.gov/pmc/articles/PMC3834504/

When my doctor placed me on antibiotics for disease treatment, I didn't know better. Then I discovered that, in order to heal, I needed to heal my gut and realized that I could never fully heal if I didn't stop taking the antibiotics. The ultimate goal was to enable my body to fight this disease on its own, not rely continuously on antibiotics. I stopped taking them and only then did I truly start to heal. But other things kill off gut flora too, such as pesticides, meat with antibiotics, alcohol, preservatives, artificial sweeteners, and chlorine and other chemicals in drinking water.

Many people experience inflammation throughout the body because of something called leaky gut syndrome. The gut has a lining that lets nutrients and particles from food and drink into the rest of the body. Poor nutrition and other factors sometimes damage that lining, letting large food particles and other substances into the blood stream that shouldn't be there. The body sees those things as foreign invaders and begins attacking them just like a virus or bacteria. That causes inflammation, which causes pain.[19] A lot of people with constant pain that's diagnosed as fibromyalgia just have a leaky gut. If they would focus on healing the gut and eating the right foods, that pain likely would lessen or even go away completely. If you experience unexplained inflammation, the first step would be to start looking at healing your gut.

I believe I may have had leaky gut. Most people do anymore because of how much we are exposed to toxic chemicals in our food and water system. It could have been adding to the pain I experienced during Lyme, which itself causes inflammation. Regardless, I knew I needed to properly heal my gut and took necessary actions to do so. First, I stopped taking antibiotics. Second, I upgraded our water filtering system. Third, I eliminated

---

19   https://www.health.harvard.edu/blog/leaky-gut-what-is-it-and-what-does-it-mean-for-you-2017092212451

inflammatory foods such as dairy and gluten. Fourth, I stopped drinking alcohol. Fifth, I started healing the gut lining by taking a glutamine supplement and drinking organic bone broth. Sixth, I started adding back in healthy bacteria through probiotic supplements, foods, and drinks.

Every day I drank (and still drink) something called kombucha, a fermented tea. You can make it on your own or purchase it from a store. Just make sure it's organic and doesn't have a lot of sugar. I also started taking a refrigerated probiotic pill daily as well. There also are many probiotic foods you can eat to increase good gut bacteria, such as sauerkraut, kefir, yogurt, kimchi, miso and pickles. With yogurt, though, you have to be really careful because many brands contain added chemicals and can be loaded with sugar!

If you truly want to improve your health, you have to start paying attention to gut health. Eliminate things that destroy healthy bacteria and consume foods and drinks that contain healthy probiotics.

Fasting

Something else I consistently came across while trying to heal from Lyme were the benefits of fasting. To be honest with you, fasting is not something I thought about doing before. It didn't make sense to me why people were doing it. Really, it has become somewhat of a trend, but a trend with some merit behind it. Once I began learning about it, the more fascinated I became and the more I wanted to learn.

Fasting has been proven to do some pretty remarkable things to the body. There are many different types of fasting. The one that I do regularly, intermittent fasting, seems to be the most popular.

types of fasting range from one day to even up to five days nger. There are even some fasting strategies that involve ng so every other day. Personally, I have never fasted for more than a day, but I have contemplated doing a three-day fast. I'm not going to get into too much detail about all the different types of fasting, though. Rather, I want to get into a little bit a detail on all the benefits, especially from intermittent fasting.

Intermittent fasting (IF) just means not eating any food for around 16 hours to an entire day. When I intermittent fast, I normally stop eating around 8 PM and then don't eat again until right around noon or 1PM the next day. It's important to still drink water during the fast.

Here are some of the benefits of IF:

1. **Decreases inflammation.**[20] This was a big one for me, someone dealing with a disease with prominent inflammation. I was doing everything in my power to reduce inflammation, which would help reduce the pain and some of the other symptoms I was experiencing.

2. **Reduces body fat, boosts metabolism, and promotes weight loss.** Studies have shown that those who followed IF for a month recorded a decrease in body fat and also lost weight.[21]

3. **Increases growth hormone (HGH).**[22] HGH plays an important role in growth, muscle strength, and metabolism.

4. **Could possibly delay aging.** One study with two groups of rats had one group fed every other day, while the other was fed every day. Interestingly enough, the group fed every

---

20   https://www.ncbi.nlm.nih.gov/pubmed/23244540
21   https://www.ncbi.nlm.nih.gov/pubmed/23244540
22   https://www.ncbi.nlm.nih.gov/pubmed/22386777

other day had an 83% longer lifespan than the ones fed every day.[23]

There are many other benefits that have been found in studies with animals, such as possibly helping with the prevention of cancer. But many of them have not undergone appropriate human testing just yet. All I know is that I have seen enough evidence to regularly follow IF myself. If you want to try out IF, again, make sure you check with your doctor to see if it's safe for you to follow.

Obtaining support from partner

Making a change in your health is a big step, since sometimes your entire lifestyle must change. Unfortunately, sometimes your partner won't necessarily support that change and this is something I come across quite often with my clients. This makes it incredibly difficult to stay committed and get results. It leads to a lot of frustration, animosity, and unnecessary arguments. Believe it or not, I've even witnessed divorces happen because of this!

There are a few reasons why issues with your partner occur when you both aren't on the same page with your new lifestyle.

First, most people get together because they relate to one another. Let's say that a couple married each other when they were both out of shape, not taking care of themselves, with low self-confidence. It's quite possible that a big reason why they connected so well stemmed from a shared lifestyle. When one person wants to change and the other doesn't, it's easy for the person who's not willing to change to fear losing the person he/she married. That fear has some merit because the only reason the person is taking these steps to change in the first place is because they

---

23   https://www.ncbi.nlm.nih.gov/pubmed/22386777

aren't happy with the person they've become, whether that's physically, emotionally, or both.

If one spouse puts effort into positive change, loses 100 lbs., gains confidence, becomes more attractive, they have in a sense become a totally different person and may not connect with or relate to their partner any longer. Believe it or not, this is quite common. Eventually, if the partner that didn't change continues to be miserable, have low self-confidence, and not take care of themselves, the couple may become distant. Once you make a positive change in your life, it's mentally exhausting to constantly be around someone who isn't willing to do the same. This is why it's so crucial to gain your partner's support and even get them to join you if they aren't currently happy with where they are in their life.

Second, it's not easy resisting temptations when your spouse purposely teases you from across the table by slowly shoving a pepperoni pizza in his or her mouth while you're eating grilled chicken and brown rice. Remember, though, that they do this because they don't want you to change and feel guilty about not making the same changes. They would rather get you to return to your old, unhealthy ways than make a change themselves. It's much easier for them to remain well inside the comfort zone they've been hiding inside for years. If you're strong-willed, though, and resist the temptations, you're liable to get frustrated with one another.

What can you do? You have to take the time for a full-on conversation with your partner about the reasons you want to make a change. You have to sit your partner down and explain to them that you are doing this for you both and your kids if you have them. It's a positive step forward that you feel you need to take to become healthier, more confident, and a better example for your children. Most people never even have this conversation, fearing that the partner will refuse to support them. What you will come to realize, though, the majority of the time you have that heart-to-heart you're going to gain your partner's support. It's the fear of not gaining support that stops people from ever having that conversation.

If after such a deep conversation, your partner refuses to support you, you have a shitty partner. There's really no other way to put it. If I sat Melinda down and told her that I wanted to make these changes to better our relationship, to be a better example to our three children, to gain self-confidence, to have a better sex life, and she looked me in the eye and told me "no, I don't support you," we wouldn't be together.

While you approach this conversation, make sure that you don't just ask for support; ask them to join you as well. Now listen, sometimes that just isn't going to happen. Take what you can get. If your spouse supports you, but doesn't want to get involved, that's OK. Just because they don't want to get involved now doesn't mean they will never get involved. It just means "not right now." Eventually, though, they will see the changes you're making and be inspired to make a change themselves.

Understanding cheat meals

Something very common that I witness often with the people I coach is that just one minor setback with their nutrition can easily lead to them completely jacking up their diet for weeks on end. For example, once they have that one slice of pizza, they think that they have completely blown their results, get frustrated, say "screw it," and proceed to devour the rest of the pie. Then that "cheat meal" turns into a cheat day and then a cheat week. They stop working out and slowly slip back into the unhealthy lifestyle they worked so hard to escape. It happens more often than you think. Maybe it's happened to you.

Cheat meals or "treat meals," whatever you would like to call them, aren't evil. For some reason, most people think they are. Many fitness coaches talk about cheat meals in a negative way. If done properly, they can actually be a very positive experience. Many peoples' experience with cheat meals end just like in the example above. Once it's planned, though, you tend to look at cheat meals much differently. As I've already talked about, you should never feel guilty about a cheat meal. If you're going to have a cheat meal, have a damn cheat meal and enjoy every bit of it! When I allow myself to go to a restaurant and indulge in a white pasta, greasy chicken parmesan with garlic bread, you better believe I'm enjoying every single moment of it and not worrying about it afterward. That's how a cheat meal should be!

So how often should you have a cheat meal? I tell my clients once a week. It's not going to affect your results. BUT it must be just one meal. It can't be a "cheat day" or a "cheat week." If your cheat meal does turn into a cheat day, you will set yourself back a bit. Just once every week allow yourself one meal where you eat what you want. Plan it and don't regret it. Once you're done with that cheat meal, though, you get your ass right back on track.

One cheat meal a week can be especially beneficial if you struggle with nutrition. For example, maybe you're someone who battles a sugar addiction. If you allow yourself one meal a week where you can have something sugary, it should satisfy your cravings long enough to get you to your next cheat meal. Or then again, maybe it won't. I've worked with some people that would rather stay fully committed to a healthy plan than have a cheat meal. They fear that if they have a cheat meal they will lose total control and revert back to the unhealthy lifestyle. You have to do what you feel is best for you.

With all that being said, though, the more you learn about healthy nutrition and recipes, you will discover that a lot of unhealthy foods can be made healthy quite easily. Take my favorite meal, chicken parmesan, for example. I can use brown rice noodles, which I believe actually taste better than regular noodles, organic pasta sauce, real cheese, and panko for the chicken breading and create a healthy chicken parmesan. Pizza is the same way. There are so many incredible healthier options available now that taste just as good as delivery pizza! My wife has done an incredible job taking unhealthy foods and creating healthy recipes for them. Make sure you follow her on social media for some of those excellent recipes. (Facebook.com/melindafitness) (IG - @CoachMelinda8)

A cheat meal is OK, but if you just want the fastest results possible and have no issue with committing to a nutrition plan, then a cheat meal might not be in your best interest. I was like that in 2008 when I began my program. I ate clean every day for 90 days, with no cheat meals. I didn't need it. If you're the same, go for it and see how many days you can commit without cheating!

For some amazing healthy recipes for some of your favorite unhealthy meals (created by my wife), be sure to head on over to www.JoshSpencer.com/book!

Understanding alcohol

I enjoy alcohol. I'm a whiskey and rum guy personally, but I don't hesitate to throw a few beers back with my buddies while watching sports games. However, I'm not that "drink a beer every night" type of guy either. Rather, maybe I'll have a few drinks during the weekend and one on date night. You need to know that alcohol has a pretty big effect on results and health.

Alcohol is normally packed with sugar and calories and slows your metabolism and protein synthesis. The metabolism slows because the body will target the alcohol for energy before it targets fat. And you don't want protein synthesis to be inhibited because it affects muscle growth. In addition, excess alcohol consumption can lead to liver issues and even certain cancer[24]. If you want great results and to stay healthy, your best bet is to eliminate alcohol consumption.

However, if you still want to throw a few back, that's fine, but you have to be smart about it. Don't shotgun a 12-pack of Bud Light three times a week and expect to have that six pack in a few months. There are some rules you need to follow. Stay away from any fruity drinks like Pina coladas. Margaritas aren't much better. Not only can they contain 60+ grams of sugar, they can be more than 500 calories a drink. If you do the math, just four of these bad boys and you're approaching the normal calorie mark for the day for most men. Beer isn't great either because it's loaded with carbs. Light beer is better, but you still want to limit how many you consume.

Like I mentioned, I'm a rum and whiskey guy, so when I go out and have a few drinks with my friends, I enjoy a rum and diet or whiskey on the rocks. I might have a vodka soda as well. Normally I'll have just a few drinks and call it quits. So, when you do drink alcohol, pay close attention to what you're consuming and how much. Be careful, too, because just one weekend full of drinks can erase an entire week of eating clean and working out.

---

24   https://www.niaaa.nih.gov/alcohol-health/alcohols-effects-body

Eliminating soda

Soda, or pop, addiction is very real. I know quite a few people who must have at least a few cans of soda a day. They are oblivious to what it's actually doing to their bodies. For one, it contains a ridiculous amount of sugar, which is linked to obesity, insulin issues, immune suppression, and many other problems. It's also an addiction. Believe it or not, studies have shown that, after consuming and stopping the consumption of sugar, rats exhibit symptoms of withdrawal similar to those of very serious drug abusers.[25]

Sodas that don't contain sugar, AKA diet soda, come filled with artificial sweeteners such as aspartame, which has been linked to a number of health issues as well, such as cancer, birth defects, diabetes, and seizures.[26] Also, soda is highly acidic, and I've mentioned the need to keep your body in a slightly alkaline state. If that's not enough to steer you in the other direction, most of sodas contain high fructose corn syrup, other chemicals, and contain no nutritional value. Basically, nothing good comes out of drinking soda other than it tastes good. You need to eliminate the use of soda as soon as possible.

Resisting temptations

I can't tell you how many times I'd be out to dinner with my family and friends when I first started my fitness journey and they would do their best to get me to eat something that went against my nutrition plan. I always refused, of course. You need to as well.

---

25   https://www.cnn.com/2017/03/02/health/sugar-brain-diet-partner/index.html

26   http://www.mercola.com/article/aspartame/hidden_dangers.htm

But most temptations don't come from others. They come from you. It's a mind game. Maybe you drive past a Taco Bell and think to yourself, "It's not going to hurt to have just one Crunchwrap Supreme." Did that just bring up nostalgic memories from drunken college nights at 2 a.m.? Just me? OK. Anyway, throughout your journey you'll be tempted to eat things you shouldn't. This is where the 10-second rule I explained earlier comes into play. Before you indulge, take 10 seconds to think about how you're going to feel. Doing that exercise in every situation like this can be the difference between average results and outstanding results. Our goal is to get you outstanding results!

Finding a support partner

When I first made a change in my health, I didn't do it alone. I asked my best friend to join me so I had someone to push me and hold me accountable. Naturally, he agreed. He's my best friend, he really didn't have a choice. He lived close by, so we worked out together every day for about a month and a half. We pushed each other and often had competitions. When you get two athletes together who hate to lose, it can be highly beneficial in a situation like this. Neither of us wanted to lose, so we pushed hard with each workout pretty much until we puked or were about to puke. Not only did we compete to see who could lose the most amount of weight the quickest, we often challenged each other to see who could get the most reps with proper form for each exercise. There was never anything left in the tank afterwards. In addition, we made a pact that neither of us would cheat on our nutrition and we checked in daily with one another to make sure.

Unfortunately, he tore his ACL playing basketball, forcing him to stop working out with me. During that month and a half, I worked out with him, though, I achieved some pretty amazing results and his accountability and support played a major role.

Fortunately, though, I had someone else supporting me as well, my coach Barbie. Like I already mentioned, Barbie helped me quite a bit, especially with nutrition, my weakest area.

It's tough to begin a journey like this alone because you are isolated from the people around you. Sometimes that's just too much for people and they give up. Having a support partner gives you a greater chance to stay committed and create a lifestyle change. You want someone who will push you, challenge you, help you, and hold you accountable with the workouts and nutrition. Your support partner can be your spouse, fitness coach (ahem), friend, or maybe someone you just met who's on the same journey.

Eating healthy at restaurants

Don't make eating out an excuse to just go ahead and blow your diet because you can eat healthy meals while eating out. Will it be as healthy as eating at home? No, most of the time it won't. The majority of restaurants want to limit costs and maximize profits, so they aren't going to spend more for organic food from suppliers. Plus, how many times have you read the menu fully enough to know the ingredients used for each meal option? You don't. Who knows what they've added. This is a big reason why I don't recommend eating out too much. But if you're on date night, vacation, or out with friends, sometimes it's inevitable. I eat out at least once a week and I'm going to teach you how to eat healthy while doing so.

It's challenging so I'm not going to try to convince you otherwise because I know just how tough it can be, even with the amount of nutrition knowledge I have. Restaurants have made it pretty damn tricky to eat healthy. You would think a salad is always healthy, right? Not so fast. With croutons, cheese, bacon, dressing, and other things added, you can easily find a salad coming in at well over 2,000 calories. Yes, you read that correctly. For some people, that's an entire day's worth of calories, all in just a salad! If you take some time to look up the nutritional value of restaurant food (there are apps for that), you'll quickly discover just how calorie-loaded most meals are and can plan accordingly. After much pressure, many restaurants have now begun listing calorie totals for their options, which definitely helps.

Here's my go-to meal when I'm eating out: grilled chicken and vegetables. You can't really go wrong with that choice. Well, you can, I guess, but most of the time you can't. You can screw it up if you load that chicken or vegetables with cheese and butter, and most restaurants do that to make it taste better. Always request no butter to be added. Be careful with the salt, too. They don't use the salt that I recommend, pink Himalayan sea salt, but just normal table salt, which isn't good for you. The sodium content of most restaurant meals is off the charts! Be sure to ask for no added salt as well.

There is another option: Bring your own food. You can always tell the waiter that you're on a strict nutrition plan for health purposes (you're not lying). Most of the time, it won't be an issue, especially if you're with a larger party. Sometimes, though, they will just tell you that you can't bring your own food. At least you tried!

Stay away from the bread and appetizers. How many times have you seen a healthy appetizer on the menu? It's pretty rare. Some of those appetizers can be more calorie-dense than the main course! Your best bet is to avoid the appetizers. And just about every place I've been to likes to bring out some sort of bread before the meal. Just politely ask them to not bring you any. It's too easy for you to indulge when it's sitting right in front of you.

If it was a healthier bread, I'd be OK with one small piece, but it's not. It's normally white bread loaded with sugar.

What can you drink? Water, unsweetened iced tea, or unsweetened green tea. That's about it. Stay away from the soda, sweet tea, and other sugary drinks.

Traveling or going out to eat with friends doesn't mean that you have to blow your diet. Just be smart about the choices you make. But don't ever use eating out as an excuse to eat unhealthy. There are plenty of different ways for you to stay on track and still go out to eat.

THE RIGHT FOODS TO EAT

It's time to really dig into the type of foods to eat, so I'm going to break down healthy foods that I consume in the categories of carbohydrates, protein, and fat. I will then share my nutrition plans for both shredding fat and gaining muscle.

Fat

We all have been programmed to believe that consuming fat leads us to being fat. Ironically enough, if you consume the right fat, the opposite occurs. Through years of research, I've learned there are many incredible benefits to having a diet rich in healthy fats. Healthy fat can reduce cholesterol, improve brain and memory function, reduce inflammation, improve digestion, help prevent cancer, protect our bodies from free radicals, and decrease the occurrence of heart disease.[27] In addition, healthy fat foods normally come chock full of vitamins, antioxidants, and other nutrients! They can provide energy too, similar to that of carbohydrates.

---

27 https://draxe.com/healthy-fats/

Once I started Lyme treatment, I increased my healthy fat intake to right around 50% of my daily calories and that's where it's still at to this day. Initially, that was just to help control inflammation, but now it's to reduce inflammation and keep me healthy, energized, and lean. Below are the healthy fats that I consume, along with the ones I try to avoid.

Healthy Fats

- Avocado

- Wild caught fish (NO farm-raised!)

- Eggs (organic pasteurized eggs)

- Almonds

- Pecans

- Walnuts

- Coconut Oil (unrefined organic virgin coconut oil)

- Butter (from raw grass-fed organic milk)

- Olives

- Extra Virgin Olive Oil

- Organic, antibiotic- and hormone-free beef

Unhealthy Fats

- Margarine

- Shortening

- Fried food

- Chips

- Candy

- Cookies

- Pizza dough

- Pie crusts

- Vegetable oils

- Carbohydrates

We have a carb problem. No, not a fat problem, a carb problem. The reason for the insane amount of health issues plaguing us today mostly results from our inability to stop consuming carbohydrates, especially sugar. Carbohydrates serve a purpose, yes, but consuming too much or the wrong type of carbs eventually leads to immune system suppression and fat gain. Nobody wants that. When I first started researching how to heal from Lyme, I constantly kept coming across books, articles, and videos talking about significantly decreasing the amount of carbohydrates consumed daily. So that's what I did. I believe it's a big reason why I've healed. Instead of consuming 50% of my daily calories from carbs, I cut it to right around 20% or less.

Before I get into good and bad carbohydrates, I want to explain exactly how they work in the body after consumption. Most people don't understand this process. It's actually quite fascinating. First, when you consume a carb, it's broken down into glucose and goes into the bloodstream. How fast it's converted into glucose depends on whether it's a simple or complex carb. Simple carbs, like sugar, digest quickly, whereas complex carbs, like sweet potatoes, digest more slowly, therefore slowly releasing glucose into the bloodstream. Once blood sugar rises, the pancreas produce insulin, "telling" the cells to take up sugar. When there is excess glucose, it's stored in the liver and muscles as glycogen. Once you burn through the glucose in the blood, the body uses the stored glycogen for energy. When the body has no more room for glycogen storage in the muscles and liver, it's converted into triglycerides and sent to the fat cells for storage.

So basically, if you consume too many carbs, your body fat increases. What's great, though, is that when the glucose and glycogen levels are low, the body will then target fat for energy. This is why so many people talk about limiting carbs while trying to lose weight. I 100% agree with them. I'm not saying completely eliminate them because they do serve a purpose. But it's important to limit how much you consume and when you consume them.

When to consume carbs remains highly controversial and people argue about it constantly. I can only share what I do and why. Basically, I like to consume healthy carbs (mostly fruits, veggies, sweet potatoes, and brown rice) earlier in the day for breakfast and lunch. I might have one small complex carb for dinner and then no carbs with my evening snack. I want to spike my blood sugar and glycogen levels earlier in the day to provide me with enough energy to get through my workouts and the rest of the day. When I decrease the amount of carbs I consume later in the evening, I tend to lose body fat a lot quicker. If you're someone trying to put on muscle, though, it's a little different. In that case, the more carbs the better. When I'm trying to put on size, I eat carbs throughout the day, even before bed.

How much carbohydrates should you consume daily? That depends on your goals and where you're currently at with your health and fitness. If you're trying to lose a significant amount of weight and body fat, I recommend around 20-30% (% of total calories) healthy carbs. If you're trying to gain mass, I recommend right around 30-40% carbs. Just know, though, that there is a fine line that varies for each individual. What I mean is that you must constantly adjust the amount of carbs you're consuming when trying to gain mass so that you don't put on too much body fat. There's a balance that only you can figure out.

When trying to gain mass, you also want to make sure you're consuming fast-digesting carbs both before and after the workout to make sure the body is not targeting muscle for energy. That will happen if there's not enough glycogen and fat to burn for energy. However, when I'm trying to lean out, I will not consume any carbs beforehand so that my body will target body fat. Does that cause muscle loss? Maybe a little, but I tend to see fat loss accelerated when I work out with depleted glycogen stores. When your goal is just to maintain, I still recommend sticking with right around 20-30% carbs.

Carb cycling is something that I do quite often that tends to lead to both fat loss and muscle gain. When I'm trying to remain super strong, but lean out at the same time, this is what I will do. What is it? It's when you increase and decrease the amount of carbs you consume each day over a certain period of time. For me personally, I like to do one day of high carbs (usually on my heavy resistance training days) and then one day of low carbs (usually on my cardio days). If I'm really trying to lean out quicker, I might do one day of high carbs and then 2-3 days of low carbs. I normally get incredible results when I follow this method. Could be something that you consider.

Healthy Carbohydrates

- Organic fruits
- Organic vegetables
- Beans
- Nuts

- Whole grains

- Legumes

- Lentils

- Brown rice

Unhealthy Carbohydrates

- Cookies

- Bagels

- White bread

- White rice

- White pasta

- Candy

- Soda

- Any products with processed sugar

Protein

The role of protein in the body is complex, but it's involved in some way with pretty much every single body function. I'm sure an entire book can be written about it, but that's not what I'm going to be doing here. I'm going to address protein in relation to fitness.

Protein is essential for muscle building and energy. Protein is made up of amino acids, which aid with muscle repair and rebuild. If you don't consume enough protein, it can throw your body into a catabolic state, which basically means that it will burn through muscle for energy. You don't want that, especially if you're trying to put on mass or even just maintain the muscle you already have. When you eat enough protein throughout the day, though, it leads to a positive nitrogen balance, therefore putting the body into an anabolic state. You build muscle when in an anabolic state.

It's important that you consume enough protein throughout the day so that you keep the body constantly in an anabolic state. There are so many differing opinions on how much protein to consume, but what I found works best for me is about 1g of protein per pound of body weight. So, if you're 170 lbs., you want to try to consume around 170g of protein per day. You can go above that, too. There's some wiggle room. I'm not exact every day, but I try to consume right around 170-220g of protein. Try to eat healthy, protein-rich foods every 2-3 hours. So, if you're 170 lbs. and eat six meals a day, try to be right around 30g of protein with each meal.

Best High Protein Foods
- Organic pasture raised eggs
- Antibiotic-free and organic chicken
- Lean, antibiotic-free, and grass-fed beef
- Organic turkey
- Wild-caught salmon
- Wild-caught swordfish
- Almonds
- Greek yogurt
- Wild-caught tuna
- Lentils

Unhealthy Protein Foods

- Farm-raised fish

- Sausages

- Hot dogs

- Fried meat

Calorie intake

My calorie intake will shift depending on my goals. If I'm trying to gain mass, for example, I will consume around 3,000-3,200 calories a day. However, when I'm trying to lean out, I will stick with around 2,000-2,200 calories a day. That is what I've discovered to be most effective for each of my own personal goals. It's taken many years of adjustments to get those numbers where they need to be. Those numbers will vary for each individual.

How you determine your calorie intake depends on quite a few different factors. First, your height and weight. Second, your goals. Third, the intensity of your workout program. Fourth, how active you are throughout the day. Fifth, your metabolism. The math is seriously complex, and I don't plan on covering it in this book. Just a simple Google search and you will be able to find tools to calculate your daily needs. However, I can talk a little bit about myself and my lifestyle to give you an idea on how I got to those numbers.

First, I'm 5'7" and normally hover right around 165-170 lbs. When I'm "bulking," I'm more around 175-180 lbs. At 165 lbs., I'm very lean with a good amount of muscle. That's my "beach weight." Normally I try to have around a 500-calorie deficit when I'm leaning out and a 500-1000-calorie surplus when gaining mass. Also, I work from home and sit behind the computer coaching others and mentoring my team on a daily basis, meaning I've got a rather inactive lifestyle. That obviously plays a factor when calculating my calorie intake. If I had a very active job, say construction for example, I would have to boost my calories. In addition, what workout program I'm going through plays a factor in how many calories I consume as well. If I'm going through an intense program where I can burn in excess of 1,000 calories per workout, I will have to increase my daily calories. If I'm going through a program where I burn just 500 calories per workout, then I won't have to adjust as much. As you can see, a lot of factors come into play.

Today, they sell watches you can wear that show the number of calories you burn throughout the day. It gets that number by monitoring your heart rate and other factors. Even if you use a tool like that, though, you're still going to have to make some adjustments. Sometimes when you start at a certain calorie number it's going to be too much, and you won't see much results. You will then have to decrease slightly until you get the number that brings steady results. Other times, you will consume a certain amount and it won't be enough. You will feel sluggish and low on energy. At that point, you want to increase slightly until you get to a point where you feel good and see results. It's tricky. To make it even more complicating, as you begin to make excellent changes and get into better shape, that number you took in before probably will have to change. When you add on muscle mass, for example, your body demands more calories. It's a lot of trial and error and constant adjustments!

Macros

Macros are just a breakdown of protein, fat, and carbohydrates. I like to keep track of my macros by percentage of total calories. There are other methods, but that's always been the easiest for me. For example, if I'm consuming 20% carbs in a 2,300-calorie diet, that means 460 calories (2,300 X .20) should come from carbohydrates. There are apps you can use that log your diet and then let you know what percentage of your calories came from fat, carbs, and protein. Every time I eat a meal, I will add that meal into the app and it allows me to know how I'm doing with my macros all throughout the day. If, after lunch, I notice that my carbs are too high and protein too low, for example, I make sure that I have a high protein, low carb dinner. At the end of the day, I want to be as close as possible to my targeted macros. Most apps will keep track of your caloric intake as well.

My macros are constantly changing, just like my calorie intake. It's no different than anything else in my life in that I have to constantly adjust. My macros before I dealt with Lyme Disease were much different than they are now. My macros when I'm trying to put on mass are much different than when I'm trying to lean out. They are always changing! When I am trying to put on mass, I will have to increase my healthy carbohydrate intake quite a bit. When I'm trying to lean out, I will have to decrease my carbohydrate intake. For the most part my healthy fat intake has stayed pretty steady regardless of my goals because of how important it is for my health.

My Complete Grocery List (Everything's Organic)

- Coconut oil
- Extra virgin olive oil
- Avocado
- Almonds
- Almond butter
- Walnuts
- Blueberries
- Strawberries
- Bananas
- Eggs
- Chicken breasts
- Turkey breasts
- Wild-caught salmon filets
- Swordfish
- Spinach

- Zucchini
- Edamame
- Broccoli
- Corn
- Peppers
- Onions
- Green beans
- Carrots
- Spaghetti squash
- Asparagus
- Sweet potatoes
- Black beans
- Pinto beans
- Brown rice
- Brown rice pasta
- Pasta sauce
- Quinoa
- Lentils
- Bragg's liquid aminos
- Oatmeal
- Ezekiel Bread
- Himalayan Salt
- Pepper
- Cumin
- Smoked paprika
- Green Tea
- Coffee

What I recommend that you do is find yourself a complete workout that comes with a nutrition plan that breaks down your macros and calorie intake.

My wife has put together a sample 1 week, 2000 calorie per day meal plan! To download it, just head over to www.JoshSpencer.com/book!

SUPPLEMENTS

The supplement market is just one big controversy. Some people swear by supplements and others believe supplements are pointless. What do I think? I think they play an important role in results if you use the right ones at the right times. Regardless of what anyone thinks, me included, the supplement market is a multi-billion-dollar industry. It's not going anywhere anytime soon because companies will keep spewing out supplements as long as demand stays strong.

Quality of supplements

I think that one of the reasons why controversy surrounds the supplement market is because of how many shitty supplements are available. I already went into good detail about the food industry and what they are doing to fool consumers. Well the supplement manufacturers do the same thing. They understand the demand for supplements and the shift toward consuming higher-quality supplements, so they purposely deceive consumers into thinking certain unhealthy products are healthy by how they label them. To make matters worse, there practically no regulations exist for the supplement market. The ingredients have to be disclosed, so that's good because that allows us to do research before we purchase anything. That is, if you take the time to do research. If you don't, I highly recommend that you start and get into the habit of doing so.

There is a big difference between good-quality supplements and poor-quality ones. Normally it's reflected in the price, but not always. Sometimes awful supplements are just as expensive as the good ones. It takes time researching to understand if it's good for you to consume or not. It's ironic to me just how many people who eat healthy and work out daily use shit supplements. It makes no sense. What you put in your body affects your health, whether that's food, drink, or supplements.

Just like with food, one of the things to really watch out for is artificial coloring. Most supplements on the market are super-bright and vibrant. That should instantly raise a red flag. There are not many natural things out there that can make a supplement neon blue. I have buddies who have said to me, "Dude, I just pissed neon green!" after using a certain supplement. No dude, that's not good.

In addition, you've got to watch out for artificial flavoring as well. Supplement manufacturers are notorious for this. Those watermelon, lemon, blueberry, raspberry, and strawberry flavored supplements more than likely are artificially created with chemicals. I shouldn't have to tell you that chemicals aren't safe to consume. Do your best to find great, high-quality supplements that are naturally flavored or unflavored. Trust me, they are hard to find, but they exist. If you can't find any, then unflavored will have to do.

If you take supplements for the taste, you're not taking them for the right reason. Quite a few different supplements that I take must be choked down, but I don't have to worry about consuming chemicals and toxins. It's either sacrifice taste now or sacrifice your health later. Again, though, this is not always the case. There are some healthy, great tasting supplements. Your best bet is to find yourself a good, high-quality supplement company and purchase the majority of your supplements through that company. Through years of research, I have found quite a few.

Pre-workout supplements

I'm a big fan of pre-workout supplements, always have been. The first supplement I ever tried, in fact, was a pre-workout supplement. If you are living under a rock and don't know about pre-workout supplements, basically they are supplements you take before your workout that boost energy. I actually went through about a five-year span trying out various pre-workout supplements to see which was best. I judged the pre-workout supplements and still do in six different areas.

1. First, the taste. Like I mentioned, it's hard to find good naturally flavored supplements and pre-workout supplements are no different. However, I have found a few and there's one in particular that I have been using before my workouts since 2015. Just because you have found one that is naturally flavored, though, doesn't necessarily mean it tastes good. Luckily, the one I use is a lemon flavor and tastes great. If I was forced to use an unflavored one, though, I would.

2. Second, I judge based on the consistency and mixing ability. I have used a lot of supplements in the past that don't mix well. I will stir and stir, but no matter how many times I do it, the supplement powder settles on the bottom of the glass. Personally, I like supplements that mix well.

3. Third, time of effectiveness. There is nothing worse than taking a pre-workout supplement that doesn't kick in until an hour and a half later. You want a pre-workout supplement to boost energy for your workouts, not afterward. I want a supplement that takes about 10-15 minutes to start working. Normally I wake up and take my supplement on an empty stomach. That actually plays a role in how quickly that supplement kicks in. If you take it on a full stomach, it will take a lot longer to be effective. Taking it on an empty stomach has always been most effective for me.

4. Fourth, the energy you have during the workout. One of the other issues I came across quite often when doing this little pre-workout experiment was that the boost I got didn't last the entire workout. Thirty minutes into the workout and I would feel drained. Great pre-workout supplements give a boost that lasts the entire workout, not just part of it.

5. Fifth, whether or not there is a "crash" afterwards. A "crash" is when you feel completely drained after your workout as if you were chased 10 miles by a bear in the woods. Some supplements I tried produced such a bad "crash" that I would almost feel sick for the remainder of the day. I felt like just crashing on the couch and doing nothing all day.

6. Last, quality of the ingredients. As I've mentioned, one of the biggest mistakes that I made early on was that I didn't pay attention to the quality of the supplements I was consuming. When I look back at some of the pre-workout supplements I used, I took a big risk. It's crucial to make sure that the pre-workout supplement that you use is void of dyes, artificial flavors, and other chemicals and toxins.

When you are looking into pre-workout supplements, I highly recommend that you judge them based on those six areas as well. I like to rank each supplement on a scale of 1-5 with 5 being the highest. It's very rare that I give 5s all across the board, but there are a few that earned that. The most important area, though, remains the quality of the ingredients. Never sacrifice quality when it comes to something you consume. If you have to spend a little extra money, then so be it. It's completely worth it for your health!

Creatine monohydrate is another supplement that I will take before my workout if I'm trying to put on mass. If I'm trying to lean out, I avoid creatine because of the water retention. Creatine draws water into the muscle cells, leading to the muscles looking and feeling fuller. That causes bloating and I'm not a big fan of feeling bloated. I don't want to look like I have a beer gut while walking on the beach. When I am focused on gaining mass and not too worried about feeling bloated, though, I like to take 2.5 grams before the workout and 2.5 grams after the workout. I mix the creatine with about 6-8 ounces of organic grape juice and take it about 15-20 minutes before the workout. The reason for the grape juice is because the creatine gets transported to the muscle cells quicker when taken with a fast digesting carbohydrate. As far as cycling goes, I like to use it for two months and take one month off. Some of the benefits of creatine include more energy during workouts, decreased muscle fatigue, and decreased recovery time. I have tried many different forms of creatine, but creatine monohydrate has worked best for me.

Glutamine is another supplement that people take before workouts. People will take it after workouts, too, but it seems to be most effective when taken before. Back in college, I used to take it after every workout and I believe it's a big reason why I was able to get so strong. Glutamine is actually the most common amino acid found in the body and levels are depleted during an intense workout. The body then goes into a catabolic state. Taking 10-15 grams of glutamine before the workout can aid protein synthesis and stop the breakdown of muscle. In addition, glutamine is very beneficial for the immune system.[28]

Intra-workout supplements

My favorite supplement that I take during my workouts is BCAAs, or branched chain amino acids. BCAAs are one of those supplements that are highly controversial, though. You will have people that will swear by them and then others who claim they are a complete waste of money. All I can do is share my own personal experience with using the supplement.

Normally when I work out, I do so on an empty stomach, with the exception of my pre-workout supplements. The only time I don't do a fasted workout is when I'm trying to put on mass. In

---

28   https://www.bodybuilding.com/content/the-benefits-of-glutamine.html

that case, I will eat a meal, wait an hour or two, and then work out. By the way, when I say "fasted workout," I mean that I haven't eaten for about 14-16 hours. I will have my evening snack around 8 PM and then not eat anything again until after my workout the following morning. When doing a fasted workout, the body likes to target muscle and fat for energy because it has no glucose or glycogen to draw from. This is good for fat loss, but you don't want to lose muscle as well. This is where I believe BCAA's really come into play. Consuming good quality BCAAs before and during the fasted workout has helped me tremendously with halting muscle loss.

I even did a little experiment. When I'm trying to lean out, I will do fasted workouts. I normally do 3 resistance workouts and 3-4 high intensity cardio workouts per week. Before using BCAAs, I noticed that I would constantly lose strength rather quickly. For example, with dumbbell bench press, I would go from doing 10 reps of 100 lbs. (each dumbbell) down to being able to do just 10 reps of 80 lbs. in just about a month. When I started taking BCAAs, I wanted to keep everything the same, including my diet, to see if I would still lose the strength. I did not. I kept the strength and, in some areas, even got stronger. Again, the only change I made was adding in the BCAA supplement. I believe BCAAs suppress protein breakdown and increase the rate of protein synthesis. Plus, they can serve as an energy source and even aid in the fat burning process. You'll just have to do your own little experiment and see if it works for you.

Post-workout supplements

I talked about there being a few times where it's OK to consume simple carbohydrates and post-workout is one of them. While you work out, you burn through your glycogen stores. That is if you're doing an intense workout. If you're doing just a very light workout, replenishing the stores really isn't that necessary. But if you work out pretty hard, you have about a 45-60-minute time frame to replenish those glycogen stores and consume enough protein to properly aid in muscle recovery. Wait too long and you will miss the window of opportunity to maximize recovery.

Fruit is actually not a good carbohydrate because it's not digested quickly enough. Rather, something like white potatoes or dextrose powder is best. I normally consume around 20 grams of simple carbs and 30 grams of protein post-workout. There are many good quality post-workout supplements on the market. And as I've already mentioned, when I'm trying to gain mass, I will also take another 2.5 grams of creatine monohydrate post workout.

Supplements before bed

I should change this to "supplement before bed" because really there's only one that I recommend, casein protein. Muscles recover most while you sleep, so consuming a slow-digesting protein like casein helps slowly supply the muscles with protein to aid in the recovery process. Normally, while bulking, I'll take 20 grams before bed.

To download a PDF of all my favorite high quality supplements, visit www.JoshSpencer.com/book

Step 3: Exercising

Exercising is important for good health. There's no denying that and there's a lot of research to back that up. It can improve your mood, sex life, brain function, energy levels, sleep, reduce chronic pain and build muscle and lose weight.[29] When trying to reach

---

29   https://www.healthline.com/nutrition/10-benefits-of-exercise#section3

your fitness goals, if you make changes to your nutrition alone you will see results. If you add in exercising daily on top of that, you will see much faster results.

Unfortunately, just like with nutrition, most people severely over-complicate it. Blame it on the media and the corrupt corporations that will do everything in their power to fool consumers. There are pills, thousands of different diets, thousands of various workout equipment, thousands of different workouts, and it makes total sense why people become so overwhelmed when trying to make a positive change in their health. But it's not complicated. It's rather simple. Just move. That's it. Move your body daily. Too many people don't move at all during the day. Rather, they get up, go to their job, which requires them to sit at a desk for 8 hours, go to lunch and sit some more, go home and sit on the couch to watch TV, and then go to bed. There is no movement! Just adding in a little bit of exercising, even just 30 minutes a day, can improve health drastically.

This section will be all about exercising. I'm going to go into detail about different workouts you can do based on your goals, what to do if you hit a plateau, how to deal with soreness, and the speed of results.

The goal of weight loss

As a fitness coach, most people come to me trying to lose weight. I'll have a few here and there who are looking to gain mass, but for the most part, they are trying to drop the pounds and body fat. I already addressed the importance of having a calorie deficit every day to lose weight, but what about the workouts? Whether you're trying to lose 10 lbs. or 150 lbs., my philosophy remains all the same. I believe that to get the best results possible, you need to have a good balance of resistance and cardio training.

I'm not a fan of just doing cardio. I don't think cardio alone will bring the best results. For one, doing strictly cardio burns a ton of muscle. If you want to look super skinny with a flat ass and without any muscle definition, then by all means go for it. But if you want to look lean, healthy, and strong, do a combination of cardio and resistance training.

I get that some people really enjoy running. My mom is one of those people. Some enjoy it so much that they do marathons. Good for them. I hate running personally, but I respect the endurance it takes to run a marathon. But at the end of the day, running alone is very tough on the body and makes people weak. Not weak as in weak-minded, but physically weak. A 30-60-minute resistance-training session one day and a 30-40-minute cardio training workout the following day finds the sweet spot for weight loss.

I want to talk about the type of cardio training that I feel is most beneficial — high-intensity interval training, or HIIT. Let me share a story. I already stated that I hate running. But there was a point when I ran 5 miles a day for my cardio. I still lifted but decided for a short period of time (about 2 months) that I would try running to see what kind of results I could get. I really didn't get any results. In fact, I had a very hard time losing body fat.

Once I started back up with HIIT, I saw results again. Maybe that was just unique to my body, but I get the best results when I'm doing HIIT for my cardio. What is HIIT? It's just like it sounds. You do short bursts of giving maximum effort followed by short bursts of slower "recovery" periods. Your heart rate constantly moves up and down, but stays high enough to help you burn much more fat than steady, low-intensity cardio. I've been recommending HIIT for cardio for years and that's what tends to bring people the best results in terms of fat loss.

What about lifting? What type of resistance training should you do? There are so many different methods, but I like to do a set of lifting exercises for a month at a certain rep count and then do a different set of exercises with a different rep count the following month. For example, I might do regular dumbbell bench press for sets of 15, 12, and 8 reps one month, and then switch to a different type of press doing 3 sets at 20, 15, and 12 reps with lighter weights the next month. Obviously, this needs to be the case with all major muscle groups, including the back, chest, arms, legs, and abs. I'm a big believer in focusing on each major muscle group once a week, meaning you need to combine some groups.

For example, maybe Monday you work the chest and abs, Wednesday the shoulders and arms, Friday the legs and back. Sunday can be your rest day. Speaking of rest days, they are important. You have to give your muscles time to recover. Taking a day off will not hurt your progress. In fact, just the opposite occurs. But mixing up the types of exercises you do and the rep counts from month to month can help you avoid a plateau and continue to see results. Many people go to the gym and do the same routines over and over again. Eventually, they reach a point where they hit that plateau. You want a set program to follow. There are tons of them out there. I can help with that if you reach out to me. But in the end, a good combination of resistance and HIIT training will help you lose the weight and reach your goals.

I do want to wrap up this section, but I need to cover one last thing. Starting an exercising program for someone who's obese and hasn't worked out in years can be extremely daunting. First of all, it's way outside their comfort zone. They fear it's going to be hard. They are right. It will be hard. Extremely hard! But as you've already learned, nothing ever gets accomplished without stepping outside your comfort zone.

Everyone, including people who have a significant amount of weight to lose, eventually must force themselves to be uncomfortable if they seek real changes. Those who work with me already understand this. The next step is finding a program or plan that won't intimidate or hurt them. It would be ridiculous if I recommended a high-intensity cardio program to someone with 150 lbs. to lose. Instead, they start out slow and work their way up to that point. For obese people, I normally recommend a program that consists of resistance training and light cardio training. If the moves are too difficult, then I have them modify where need be. The goal is to get them to move and consistently challenge themselves. As they get stronger and lose the weight, they can slowly start adding in more difficult and more intense exercises.

The goal of gaining mass

Gaining mass is a lot more difficult than losing weight. Well, I guess it's not really that much more difficult, but it just takes longer, sometimes a lot longer. If you think you need patience to lose weight, you'll need even more patience to gain mass. The most mass I've ever gained in a three-month time period is 11 lbs. I gained that without increasing body fat. That's practically unheard of. The only reason why I believe I could gain that amount in a short amount of time was because of muscle memory, my body type, and creatine monohydrate.

I'm a fitness coach. I work out all the damn time and have since I started college in 2003. Once you have built muscle before, it tends to come back much quicker than for someone who has never lifted a day of his life. Plus, with my body type, I tend to put on muscle rather easily. After I went through Lyme treatment, I was skinny as a rail. I started a very intense lifting regimen and put the muscle back on rather quickly. And again, creatine monohydrate probably played a role in that as well. Remember, creatine draws water into the muscle cells. Sure, I definitely gained a lot of strength in those three months, but some of the weight could have been from a little bit of water retention as well. Regardless, patience is key when you're trying to put on size.

Let me dig a little deeper on the different body types. Basically, there are three main body types:

Ectomorphs: Ectomorphs are the hard-gainers I talked about. They are naturally skinny and lose fat extremely easily, but have a real tough time putting on muscle. These are your buddies who can shove their faces full of pizza all day every day without gaining a pound. In order to put on mass, they need to eat a ridiculous number of calories.

Endomorphs: Endomorphs are people who put on weight and muscle very easily, but have a tough time losing the weight once they put it on.

Mesomorphs: Mesomorphs are sort of middle of the ground. They put on muscle pretty easily and can lose body fat fairly easy as well. I'm a mesomorph.

Regardless of your body type, you shouldn't do too much cardio when you're trying to gain mass. You need the calories and doing too much cardio burns too many calories. Endomorphs can get away with a little more cardio, though, because of how their bodies store fat. Two or three cardio sessions per week should be fine. Ectomorphs should especially limit their cardio, though, to right around one or two 30-minute sessions per week. Some don't do cardio at all when trying to put on size. When I'm trying to gain mass and stay somewhat lean (as a mesomorph), I do two cardio sessions per week, and those sessions are rather light. I don't want to do many high-intensity cardio sessions because it burns too many calories and is tougher to recover from.

Resistance training should be the focus when trying to put on size. I pretty much will do the same type of lifting routines and mix them up like I mentioned, but I try to stick with lower rep counts. The most reps I do for any given set is 15. There's no reason for me to go into detail about the exact exercises to do. Instead, that's what you need to reach out to me about. Once again, I can recommend an entire program for you to follow.

Dealing with a plateau

I've got news for you. There will be moments along your journey when you hit a plateau. It's inevitable. Don't bitch about it, don't mope around, don't use it as an excuse to blow your nutrition plan. Just deal with it! Once again, the only path to success is full of constant peaks and valleys. Success with your health is no different. Once you hit that first plateau, figure out what adjustments you can make so that you can continue moving forward. Sound familiar? It should. I covered the hell out of this routine earlier in the book.

But why does a plateau occur? Many times, it has everything to do with calories consumed and macros. However, doing the same damn workout over and over again without switching things up can also bring on a plateau. When you do resistance training, you are actually tearing tiny muscle fibers, which explains the soreness after workouts. You tear muscle fibers, but then the body repairs and rebuilds them to make them stronger. That's how muscles grow and you gain strength.

However, when you settle into a routine and do the same exercises repeatedly, you no longer tear the muscle fibers. This is why it's always crucial to mix up your workouts and exercises. Most men are stubborn and do the same routine over and over again at the gym. I used to be one of those men. Eventually I changed things up and found a new program because I got so tired of not getting results. But if you're one of those people who can't get results doing the same routine at the gym, it's time to think outside the box and make some changes. Do some research, watch videos online, find yourself a coach. There are thousands of different options and schedules you can follow that can help you continuously experience results.

There are other factors that come into play, though, when someone experiences a plateau. Not only could it be that they are doing the same routine too often, not eating enough, or don't have the proper macros, but they could be overtraining or dealing with a health issue. One of the problems I come across often with the people I coach is that they don't consume enough calories. In their minds, if they eat less they will lose weight faster. It's important to have a calorie deficit if you want to lose weight, yes, but if you take it to the extreme you won't lose any weight at all. Your brain is very smart. If you're not consuming enough calories, your brain will send a message to your body to begin storing fat. It thinks there is a famine and throws your body into what is called starvation mode. You simply can't burn fat while you're in starvation mode. It doesn't matter how much you work out, how great your calorie deficit is, your body will hold onto that fat for dear life.

Another issue is overtraining. I come across this rarely, but it does occur. I've only over-trained once in my life. My dumb ass tried to do three workouts a day while consuming 1,800 calories. Obviously, this was well before I knew better. Eventually it got to the point where I got so sick and so exhausted that I couldn't function for about three days. My body just completely shut down. I had to take an entire week off from working out. Once I started feeling better, I quickly adjusted the calories I consumed and went back to working out once a day. Be smart about what you're doing and listen to your body.

Health issues can slow or stop results as well. I've known quite a few people who have been really strict with their nutrition and worked out daily and can't lose the weight. For some reason, their bodies will signal fat storage when it shouldn't. In my experience, a few reasons may trigger this. It could be that their hormones are all out of whack. Could be a thyroid that's jacked up, or stress. Thyroid issues will signal the body to do the opposite of what it should do, so when you are doing everything right to lose weight, it will "say" to the body "nope, let's store fat." And when you're stressed out, the body produces cortisol, which slows down the metabolism and shuts down digestion.[30]

The best thing to do if you think your hormones are behind your plateau is to first get proper thyroid testing done. Ask to test the TSH, free T3 and T4, TPO, and anti-thyroglobulin antibodies.[31] With stress, you just have to get it under control. I know that anxiety, fear, and other factors come into play, but you have to take everything that I taught you earlier in the book about mindset and apply it. Getting that stress under control is crucial! If you have to do meditation daily, do it. If you have to get massages weekly, do it.

But the second health reason behind not losing weight could be an underlying disease. Lyme messed up my body. It messed up my nutrition levels, thyroid, cholesterol, liver, and kidneys. When

---

30   https://drhyman.com/blog/2016/08/05/how-to-fix-your-hormones-and-lose-weight/
31   https://drhyman.com/blog/2016/08/05/how-to-fix-your-hormones-and-lose-weight/

the body deals with chronic inflammation like you experience with Lyme, it tends to focus all of its attention on reducing that inflammation. If you think you might be dealing with a disease, go find a good doctor and get properly tested.

Speed of results

You have to be extremely patient when it comes to getting results. Normally, people lose about 1-2 lbs. per week with a good workout routine and a clean diet at about a 500-calorie deficit. However, that varies from person to person. If you're a former athlete who has a lot of experience working out in the past, for example, results will more than likely come quicker for you because of muscle memory.

On the flip side, if you're someone who has no experience with working out, chances are it's going to take you much longer to see results. I have noticed, though, that the more weight you have to lose, the faster the weight comes off, at least initially. Eventually, everyone hits that point where the results slow down. Regardless, patience is key. Give it time. If you're doing the right things day-in and day-out, results will come.

Soreness and rest

If you're someone who hasn't worked out before and start a new workout routine, you're in for one hell of a surprise in your first few weeks. You're going to experience a level of soreness that you've never experienced before! Even those with some sort of past with exercising, if you took a long break, you're going to be sore as well. Just expect it. When I forget to tell my clients about the typical soreness that accompanies a program, they come back to me a few days after they start almost in a panic, thinking they seriously injured themselves. I get the "I can't move my arms" comment quite a bit.

The more you work the muscles, the less sore you will become. Eventually, it will get to the point where you experience only minor soreness after each workout. So most of the time when people come to me worried, it's just normal muscle soreness. But on a rare occasion, it can be an injury as well. If you think you have injured yourself, it's important to see a doctor immediately. If it's not an injury, it's not going to hurt to continue working out while being sore.

Proper rest will reduce soreness. Most people hate taking a rest day, me included. I'd rather work out every day. If I don't work out, I feel lazy and unproductive. However, those rest days play an important role in muscle recovery. Taking a day off every single week can help reduce soreness by letting the muscles heal. After the rest day, you should be ready to get back to your workouts again.

If you want your muscles to heal, you need to get a good amount of sleep each night. Believe it or not, the body recovers the most when you sleep because the body releases growth hormones, which aids in muscle repair and recovery. If you are trying to gain mass, it's important to eat a high protein meal or snack before bed. During sleep, the body actually goes catabolic. Eating before bed, though, discourages that from happening. Plus, getting a good night's rest makes you energized and alert when you wake up, helping you crush your workouts. Try to get at least 7-9 hours of sleep each night, especially while going through a rigorous workout routine.

Financial Success

ARE YOU STRUGGLING financially? It's OK if so. Well it's not OK, but just because you're struggling currently doesn't mean you can't get it under control. Most people don't have their finances under control. That's a reality of the world we live in. For some odd reason, we've gotten to this point where people like to spend more than they have. It's become an acceptable part of society. It shouldn't be, though. They believe that just because they have credit cards they can purchase what they want, even if they can't afford it. It's true, it allows them to purchase what they want, but it doesn't come without repercussions.

It all goes back to the instant gratification mindset. People are quick to think, "I want this now, so I'm going to purchase it," not looking ahead and comprehending the 20%+ APR they will pay on the balance each month. That adds up quickly, as you might have already come to realize.

In addition, most people don't have a clue how to properly manage and structure their finances. They are all over the place and utterly disorganized. They don't know their income and expenses and what is left over (or not left over) at the end of each month. Basically, they just don't know what they are doing and spend recklessly.

I'm fortunate to have been raised in a family that had the finances under control. Most people aren't that lucky. I'm also fortunate that I have the knowledge of properly managing finances because of my schooling and short stint as a financial advisor. Combine those and, no matter what our current income has been over the years, we've been able to manage our money successfully. Sure, there were times we were really, really struggling, as you discovered earlier in the book. But even during those times, we knew how much money we had coming in and going out, and never spent more than we had. We never allowed ourselves to have credit card debt. We had and still have full control over our finances.

I'm going to teach you how to gain control of your finances. I'm going to teach you how to think outside the box and earn more income. I'm going to teach you how to create financial freedom, which we all desire. This will be a step-by-step process, so pay close attention to this section. Let me teach you how to have financial success.

STEP 1: CREATE A BALANCE SHEET

Do you know your expenses? Do you know your income? You probably do know your income because you cash that check each week, but chances are you have no idea what you're spending. You probably also have no idea whether you have a positive or negative cash flow each month. We have to get you organized. If you're not organized, you're not going to be able to get your finances under control and create financial success.

Becoming organized is not difficult. Even if you aren't "good with numbers," anyone can do it. Sit down with your partner, open up an Excel spreadsheet, or even grab a pen and notepad, and create two columns: one for your income coming in and one for your expenses.

With your income, make sure you include both your salaries, wages, or any other income that might be coming in on a monthly basis, such as from your investments, if you have any. With the investments, though, only include the ones that are providing immediate cash flow. Those that are tied up in retirement accounts, such as with a 401K or IRA, you can't include because you don't have access to that money until a certain age, unless you want to pay a hefty fee for early removal.

With your expenses, make sure you include car payments, house payments, student loans, utilities, groceries, gas, credit card debt, miscellaneous spending, etc. Include everything that you're spending money on each month. Here's a good habit to get into, at least until you gain control of your finances. Start asking for receipts (even if you use a debit or credit card) for every single purchase you make and place those receipts in a container. At the end of each week, take just a few minutes and add up those receipts. Chances are you're spending much more than you realized and probably need to.

But once you have both your total income and expenses written down, total them up. If your income is greater than your expenses, that's a good start. If your expenses are greater than your income, we have some work to do.

If you feel like you're living "paycheck-to-- paycheck" you're going to have to make some adjustments. Even if you have a positive cash flow after expenses, but still feel like you're cutting it close each month, we have to get you to either reduce expenses or increase income. Right now, I'll focus just on reducing expenses because I'll address increasing income in a bit.

To reduce expenses, you will have to get creative. When Melinda and I were struggling financially, we had to get very creative to create a positive cash flow each month. With groceries, for example, we looked at every opportunity possible to reduce what we were spending on food. One idea we came up with was to purchase the majority of our food in bulk for the month instead of single items at a time. Purchasing food in bulk is much cheaper than purchasing items individually and saved us quite a bit each month. We also looked at the amount of times we went out to eat. Eating out at restaurants is expensive. We stopped eating out completely and that move alone led to a pretty drastic increase in cash flow.

In addition, we looked in depth into our unnecessary spending on little things. For example, we used to get coffee quite regularly at Starbucks. We only went a few times a week, but if we both got coffee we were spending around $8 each time, which included a tip. If we went twice per week, that was $16 a week or $64 a month. By drinking coffee at home, that was an extra $64 we held onto. The crazy part about this is that most people get coffee daily. If they go 5 times per week and spend $3 per coffee, that's $60 a month they could be saving by making their own coffee at home. That's $60 that can be applied to credit card debt or car or house payment.

In addition, start making conscious decisions with your utilities. It's not necessary to have the house set at 64 degrees in the summer. Instead, you could set the AC at 70 and still be comfortable. The same goes with the heat in the winter months. And start paying attention to the amount of water you're using, too. You can easily take a 4-minute shower, rather than a 15 minute one. Just those changes alone can save you quite a bit of money each month.

Every bit counts when trying to create a positive cash flow. If you go through everything you're spending money on each month, I can almost guarantee you that you'll find quite a few other things that just aren't necessary. You might be able to save hundreds a month by eliminating unnecessary spending.

STEP 2: CREATE SEPARATE ACCOUNTS

Most people spend recklessly. They will buy things without considering how it affects their bottom line each month. What's interesting is that most people increase their spending when their income increases. I've known a lot of people who bring in a fairly significant amount of income, but yet still live paycheck-to-paycheck. There is no reason why someone making a six-figure income should still have a negative cash flow, but yet it happens quite regularly. No matter how much or how little money you make, I want you to create separate bank accounts for savings, expenses, "play money," and donations. This will keep you organized.

Sit down with your partner and look at your balance sheet. Once you have a good understanding of your income and expenses, you need to figure out what percentage of your weekly income you can allocate for savings, "play money," everyday expenses, and donations, if you want to do them. After creating separate bank accounts for each of these, each week, after you get your paycheck, you put a specified amount of that money into each account. For example, let's say your weekly combined paychecks total $1,000. After sitting down with your spouse, you both concluded that 40% needs to go toward expenses, 20% will go toward savings, 5% will go towards donation, and the remaining 35% will be for "play money." You then take $400 ($1,000 x .40) and put it into your expenses account, $200 ($1,000 x .20) and put it into your savings account, $50 ($1,000 x .05) and put it into your donations account, and $350 ($1,000 x .35) and put it into your "play money" account. At the end of each month, you will have added $1,600 ($400 x 4) into your expenses account, $800 ($200 x 4) into your savings account, $200 ($50 x 4) into your donations account, and $1,400 ($350 x 4) into your "play money" account.

If you're a business owner, you can't forget about taxes either. For many of us, our taxes are not automatically taken out of our checks each month, unless you have hired a payroll company or accountant to do so. That means we have to allocate a certain percentage of our income toward taxes. From day one of opening my business, that percentage has been 35%. Did I need it to be that high when just starting a business? No, but I'd rather be safe than sorry. The last thing I want is a tax bill for well more than I planned it would be. Plus, there are tax perks of being a business owner, such as write-offs, which bring down the amount of income you pay taxes on. If, at the end of the year, I only have to pay 20% taxes when I planned for 35%, that means I have an extra 15% sitting in my account I can either invest, save, or donate.

After creating these separate accounts and allocating your money into them, you are not allowed to cross the accounts with your spending. For example, if you use up all $1,400 from your "play money" account before the month ends, you can't allow yourself to dip into your savings account for more "play money." The play money account is for play money only. The savings account is for savings only and so on and so forth. This is a simple idea that can have a drastic effect on your cash flow! This will keep you organized.

STEP 3: PAY OFF YOUR CREDIT CARD BALANCE EACH MONTH

Credit card debt is more than likely the reason why you feel like your finances are a sinking ship. Again, most credit cards charge around 20% interest on the balance. That's a lot. Think of it this way. If you have $10,000 in credit card debt, if the APR (annual percentage rate) is 20%, that's $2,000 in interest every single year. Wow. If you're paying just the minimum balance each month, it can quickly spiral out of control, as you can see. You can't just ignore the interest rate. Nothing ruins finances quicker than credit card debt. From this point forward, you have to do everything in your power to quickly pay down that debt.

If you currently have a large amount of credit card debt, say $10,000, you are more than likely not in the financial position to pay off that debt immediately. However, you need to pay down and eliminate that debt as quickly as possible. What you could do is dedicate a specific amount of your weekly income towards the credit card debt and include it in your expenses account. For example, continuing with the previous example, maybe you quickly discover that you don't necessarily need $1,400 a month for "play money." You can get by with just $700 per month. So, then you would change your allocation percentages accordingly, taking that $700 and putting it into your expenses account, which you will dedicate solely towards paying down your credit card debt. In just a short amount of time, you will be able to completely eliminate that debt.

If you have quite a bit of credit card debt, you might want to attempt to negotiate with your creditor to get that percentage down. You'd be surprised, many times they will work with you. Even if it's just a 1% decrease in the APR, that means you can pay off the debt quicker.

Once you fully eliminate the credit card debt, you have to get into the habit of paying off your credit balance every month. This must be a priority, no exceptions. This is one of the things my parents taught me when I was very young. In all the years I have had a credit card, I have never once had to pay interest because I have always paid the balance each month. This should be non-negotiable for you from this point forward.

Step 4: Pay Bills on Time

There's not much that confuses me more than someone who pays their bills late every month who can actually afford to pay their bills on time. When you pay your bills late, you also have to pay fees. Those fees add up. I've known people over the years who pay well over $200 a month in late fees! That's ridiculous. If you're struggling financially, this just can't happen. If you become organized and follow the method I've outlined above, you now should be able to have the money you need in your expense account to properly pay your bills each month. Don't be late on your payments. Do automatic withdrawal if you have to. If you take this route, though, be sure to check your bills each month to make sure they're correct. If you don't want to do automatic withdrawal, make sure you set it up so that you get email or text notification when your bill comes due. Doing this, along with paying off your credit card, will help with your credit score, which plays a big role in whether or not you get a loan and your interest rate for that loan. The better your credit, the better the rates, which saves you money, sometimes quite a bit over time.

Step 5: Don't Add Any More Debt

I would assume that this would be obvious for those who are struggling financially, but I've learned not to assume anything.

If you are trying to pay down and eliminate your debt, don't add any additional debt. That makes no sense.

STEP 6:– CHANGE YOUR TRIBE

I was on a trip in San Diego with a highly successful buddy of mine and after a few drinks we started having a conversation about his "tribe" back at home, or the people he's around the most. He began talking about how he enjoys being around me and our circle of friends because we are always so positive, laid-back, business-minded, have our shit together, and help him become a better all-around person. However, when he started talking about his friends back home, his tone changed. He got this sad look on his face as he explained the lack of support they give him and how they constantly drain his energy. I told him that he needed to change his "tribe" quickly or else he would be constantly held back.

People are either energy givers or takers. Energy givers make you feel great, support you, encourage you, challenge you, always want to progress on a personal level, and consistently guide you into becoming a better person. Energy takers, or what I like to call energy vampires, drain the energy right out of you. When you are around energy vampires, you feel sad, negative, sometimes almost depressed, and know deep down in your gut that you shouldn't be hanging around them, but you still do. These are the people who don't support you, are quick to tear you down, always gossip about others and sometimes even you, have no desire to move forward in life, and constantly bitch about the terrible situation they're in financially, physically, and/or emotionally without putting in any effort to change.

I want you to do something for me right now. Think about your five closest friends. Next, ask yourself if these five people currently have a positive or negative influence on your life. "Oh shit," right? Next, I want you to think about those of your friends who you know will join or support you as you begin to make changes in your life and those who won't. As tough as it is to do, if you have friends who currently affect you negatively or who you know won't be a good influence as you try to move forward, it's time to shy away from them. I'm not saying you have to shut them out completely, but just take a step back with how much time you spend with them. Constantly being around those who are negative will do you no good.

Think of it this way. If your current circle of friends struggles financially and are financially irresponsible, it's easy for you to be as well. You have to surround yourself with people who are currently where you want to be. If you want to be debt free, grow your income, understand investing, then you have to be around people who are debt free, successful entrepreneurs, and smart investors. My circle of friends consists of people who are better than me and challenge me daily to do greater things with my life. They are a big reason why I've been able to make so much progress and accomplish what I've been able to accomplish thus far in my life, especially in a business and financial sense. They give me energy, not take it away. They help me become better, not worse.

Now listen, I get it, making new friends is hard. When we moved to Texas, we discovered that fairly quickly. What makes this even more challenging is the fact that most people are energy vampires, not energy givers. It's tough finding those gems who provide the positive influence you need. But you must try to find them. They will have much more of an impact on your life than you can imagine. If you have one friend who is successful, maybe you make more of an effort to hang around their friends as well. Successful people understand the importance of hanging around other successful people, which might give you an opportunity to make better friends. This happened with me. I started out becoming very good friends with successful people and eventually met their friends. Then we all became very good friends. Because of this happening repeatedly, our network or "tribe" of successful, positive people grew quite drastically over the years. In fact, I met my buddy I was talking about in the beginning of this section through another successful friend.

Starting today, it's time that you find your "tribe." It's time to surround yourself with people who are going to have a positive influence on your life instead of a negative one. Don't take this lightly, either. It's much more important than you think!

STEP 7: FIND WAYS TO INCREASE YOUR INCOME

Just a bit ago, I discussed how to reduce expenses to begin gaining control of your finances, but there's a good chance that you still don't have enough cash flow coming in to truly get to where you want to be. Your current income sources might be providing you enough to function, but they probably aren't allowing you to do what you need to do to create a better lifestyle, reduce and eliminate debt quickly, and invest at the pace you need to generate real wealth. I hate to be the bearer of bad news, but having a positive cash flow of, say, $100 per month is not nearly enough, especially if you have a lot of debt. That's why you need to look into different ways to increase your income.

Many people have big financial goals. I truly believe that most people strive to be financially independent. You might (and should) be one of those people. However, you have to take a step back, look at yourself in the mirror, and ask "Am I doing everything in my power to move towards my financial goals?" There's a good chance you're not. Remember, you can't expect different results if you continue to do the same things over and over again. Too many people get stuck in this exact scenario, mostly because of their fear of change, which I discussed earlier in the book. It's hard to change because change is uncomfortable. But change is necessary if you want different results. If you want to get out of debt, improve your lifestyle, and create wealth, reality is that you're going to have to do something different than what you're doing now.

The number one reason I became a business owner was to have control over my money and my time. When I worked for someone else, that wasn't the case. Plus, I wanted to be able to completely eliminate my debt and have a substantial amount of money to invest to create true wealth for my family and me. On a fixed income, it would have taken me many, many years to make that happen. After starting my own business and through an incredible amount of effort, I created a significant income, paid off all my debt, and invested a lot of money toward our and our children's future in a rather short amount of time.

At this very moment, I want you to be real with yourself. There are a few questions I want you to take some time to think about. Maybe even discuss these with your spouse.

- Are you passionate about your career choice?

- Is your job giving you time freedom?

- Is your job making you enough to have a positive cash flow each month?

- Is your job making you enough to invest?

- Are you currently making enough for a comfortable lifestyle?

- Is your current job creating passive (residual) income?

- Are you thinking outside the box to create additional cash flow for your family?

If you answered "no" to any of these, it's time for you to make some changes. If you answered "no" to most or all of these, then you absolutely *have* to make some changes.

WHY STARTING A SIDE BUSINESS IS A GOOD IDEA

If your career is not making you happy, not providing you with enough cash flow to enjoy life, travel, pay down debt, and invest, then you either look for a new career or start up something on the side that can either supplement or even possibly eventually replace your current income. Personally, I'm a big advocate of starting a side business because then you can control your income and time. Switching jobs to something that you finally enjoy, while still working for Corporate America is better, but that still doesn't address the issue that you don't have full control over your income and time. Whether you think so or not, you don't have full control. You want something where you do have full control.

Let me explain. When you run your own business, at least you have control over whether or not your business fails (for the most part), mostly depending on your effort and your ability to overcome failure and make quick adjustments. Because I own and run my own business, the success or failure of the business and my income is dependent on me. When working for Corporate America, though, your company can fire you at any time. They can also demote you if they want. And if the company goes under, you're left scrambling to find a new job. The worst part about it, though, is that your pay normally doesn't match your effort. Your company and boss determine how much you're worth and what you get paid. *You* are the only one who can determine what you're worth and what you should get paid! Why are you letting someone else dictate that part of your life?

I'd rather control what happens with my income. Look at it this way. Let's say there's employee A and employee B. Both work in a typical corporate setting. Employee A is highly motivated, has a great work ethic, is super positive, shows up to work early, and always comes up with incredible ideas to help the company move forward. Employee B on the other hand, is as lazy as it comes. He shows up late, only does what he's asked, badmouths his bosses and company, and finds ways to "cheat the system," like taking a 30-minute dump while browsing Instagram on company hours.

Employee A obviously has a better chance of moving up in the company, but by how much and who controls it? Most certainly not the employee. His boss is in full control. If he does "move up," he might get a $5,000 raise every two years. Cue the sad music. The odds of him ever reaching the "top" are pretty slim. Oh, and that lazy employee B, he is making just a little less than you per year. How does that make you feel? Here you are working maybe two to three times as hard as employee B, but you're only making slightly more than him. It's not fair. Unfortunately, this is a very common scenario.

Let's take it even further. Let's say that employee A actually does make it to one of the top positions in his company. Awesome, right? Not really. His income is still severely limited. Maybe he makes $250,000, which is a lot, sure, but what if his earning potential on his own is $2 million a year? If he has the type of work ethic and ambition to get to $250,000 a year and to the top of his company, there's a great possibility he could make $2 million+ per year with his own business. That's not even considering the hours he has to work to sustain that $250,000 income. The time sacrifices he makes are probably astronomical. If his son has a ball game, he's more than likely the guy who says, "sorry son, I can't make your game today because I have to work." What is the point of making that type of money if you can't even enjoy life? That's Corporate America.

To make it worse, his income is tied to his time. If he stops working, the money stops coming in. Too many people don't understand the power of residual or passive income. I encourage you to change you're thinking about this. What is passive income? Passive income is simply money that is earned without having to put in much effort. Dividends, real estate investing, affiliate or network marketing, creating online courses, are all examples of passive income.

Here's another way to look at it. I know a lot of personal trainers. Personal training is a tough career because income is entirely dependent on the number of hours that the trainer can train his clients. If he stops training, he stops getting paid. I know some people who work their ass off, but only make about $30k-$40k per year. Whenever I come across personal trainers, I do my best to help them see the opportunity to create passive income. They can become an affiliate for a supplement company, create their own YouTube channel sharing various exercises, create and sell an online personal training course, or even become involved in a network marketing company that specializes in fitness programs and supplements. All of these would provide an excellent opportunity for them to earn additional income without putting in too much effort.

Right now, you should start thinking about the different ways that you can create passive income. Think about all the things that you're passionate about, things you enjoy doing. Think about your strengths. You never want to start something on the side that aren't any of these things. If you try to start something that you're not passionate about, for example, you'll never be able to make it successful. I wrote this book because I love to write, I'm passionate about every topic I discuss, and all of these areas are strengths of mine. You've got to dig deep and think about what opportunities can arise from your passions, strengths, or even hobbies. Write your ideas down, do some research, figure out which opportunity would be the best for you and your family, and then take action. This is another one of those things where you can't wait. You need to take action immediately.

Controlling income is important, but controlling your time is everything. I know many very wealthy people who don't have control of their time. It doesn't matter how much money you make, if you aren't able to experience time freedom you have nothing. What good is money if you aren't able to enjoy experiences with your loved ones and friends? What good is it if you can't even make it to your son's baseball game or daughter's dance recital? What good is it if you're limited to just one or two vacations per year? It's worthless. Nobody wants to work their life away.

Unfortunately, this happens too often. And then you have people with loads of money lying on their deathbed regretting working their entire lives and missing out on amazing experiences. The goal is for you to have total income *AND* time freedom. If I want to take a break and spend time with my kids, I do. If I want to just pick up and go on a snowboarding trip on 3 days' notice, I will. If I want to take 12 trips a year, I can do so. If I want to take my family on a vacation, I don't have to ask my boss if it's OK. There's a great chance that right now your current situation doesn't allow you time freedom.

With all that being said, though, there are people who aren't geared for owning their own business. There are also people that have no desire to do so. They might enjoy their careers. A lot of careers out there are high-paying and incredibly rewarding and fulfilling. Great! At minimum, though, if you are struggling financially, need to reduce debt quickly, and want to have more spending money, you're going to have to at least do something on the side. If you want to keep it as a side gig, that's fine. You don't have to build it to possibly replace your current income. Maybe you enjoy your career so much that you just don't want to. However, there are many people who do have the desire for their part-time job to replace their full-time career. It all goes back to what exactly you want.

Different types of business opportunities

Everything I just mentioned should motivate you to begin looking for additional opportunities. You want to control your money and time. My advice is to start a side business and work hard with it when you can, all while keeping your current job to sustain enough income to support your family. Does that mean you will have to make time sacrifices? Of course. But make those sacrifices and put in as many hours as possible so that you have the opportunity (if you want to) to possibly quit the job that you don't enjoy and make your part-time business your full-time career.

There are many, many opportunities out there. You just have to put a little effort into it and talk to the right people to find them. It's important, though, that you research everything. It's no different than researching ingredients while at the grocery store to discover if the product is healthy or not. You have to research whatever opportunity you're contemplating or product or service that you're thinking about creating to find out if it's legit and if it's a good fit for you. Trust me when I say there are a lot of bad opportunities out there. In addition, there are a lot of excellent salespeople who will make bad opportunities look like good ones.

You have to be able to sort through the bullshit and discover the truth. Never feel bad for taking your time to research and talk to others to see if an opportunity is the right one.

There are many different types of opportunities available to help you create time and financial freedom. In addition, again, whatever you do, you want to be able to create passive income. I can spend quite a bit of time going over the numerous amounts of opportunities, but I'm not going to. Instead, I'm going to briefly hit on a few, just to get your wheels spinning.

Network marketing, the career choice I got into back in 2008, is one of those opportunities. Network marketing is great because you can become a business owner quickly with minimal start-up costs and, for the most part, have control of your income. Plus, it's one of the best opportunities to create passive income because of the team-building aspect of the business. It works if you find the right company. I was able to create a million-dollar-plus income per year from it. It has served as a great income source to create other avenues of income. In my next book, I'm going to go into extreme detail about how to successfully build a network marketing company, so be on the lookout for that!

However, network marketing has its downfalls. For one, you really don't have total control. The company you decide to join still creates the products, determines the compensation plan (which they can change at any time), or can decide to sell the company and shut down the network in a moment's notice. I've been around in network marketing long enough to, unfortunately, see this happen to quite a few companies, leaving their distributors stranded. So yes, network marketing can be great if you find a great company, but there are downfalls as well, just like with anything else.

Real estate investing is another way to create passive income and build serious wealth. Many people have gotten into real estate investing in recent years because of all the TV shows making it look so easy. It's not easy. Starting up any business isn't easy. You have to be willing to struggle and go through a lengthy learning curve to figure it out. In addition, real estate investing has everything to do with numbers. You have to quickly run projections when an opportunity to purchase a property opens up. You have to make smart buys.

In my opinion, the best way to create real wealth with real estate is to buy a property with great potential in the right neighborhood where house prices are appreciating, fix it up, and then rent it out. If you do it right, not only will you create a positive cash flow each month (rent minus expenses), and you also will be paying down the mortgage and building equity, all while the property value increases each year. In my opinion, real estate provides the greatest opportunity for serious returns, especially long-term. There's a reason why so many millionaires invest a ton of money into real estate.

The last one I'll briefly address is creating online courses. If you have enough knowledge in an area where you feel you can help a lot of people, this might be an option for you. There's quite a learning process that you will have to go through, though, especially if you don't have any prior knowledge of marketing. You will have to successfully and professionally create the course and market it specifically to the people who will benefit from it most. Social media marketing (advertisements) is probably the best route for marketing currently.

RELATIONSHIP SUCCESS

You EVER LOOK back to when you were in your late teens and early twenties and think to yourself "what in the world was I doing back then?" I do all the time with pretty much every aspect of my life. When I focus on my relationships specifically, though, I want to face-palm.

Over the years, though, through many personal experiences and a lot of personal development, I feel I have gotten to a great place with my relationship with my wife, kids, and friends. I'm not anything like I was back then. I have been able to mature in so many ways. Once again, I believe it has to do with my ability to realize that there is always room for improvement.

I have taken the same approach with my relationships as I have with my mindset, health, and finances. I am constantly going through my 5-step failure process and correcting my mistakes. I've made a lot of them and you probably have as well. That's OK. There's nothing wrong with making mistakes with your relationships as long as you're willing to make whatever changes necessary to improve. Don't be that stubborn asshole who believes that everything you do is right. That's a great way to chase away the people you care about most.

When I take a step back and look at relationships in general, they are in turmoil. There are a hell of a lot of terrible spouses, friends, and parents out there. Divorce rates have skyrocketed, there is complete disconnect between parents and their kids, and friends are stabbing each other in the back like never seen before. Establishing great relationships is one of my strengths and this section is going to be dedicated to teaching you how I've been able to establish such an incredible relationship with my wife, three kids, and all of my friends. I hope this helps. And just like with every other section, take what you learn here and apply it immediately. I'm going to help you better your relationship with everyone in your life!

HOW TO BE A GOOD SPOUSE

This isn't just for spouses. If you are an unmarried couple that's fine too, but this section is strictly for your relationship with your significant other. There are a lot of terrible spouses out there and it's disgusting to watch so many people cheat on each other, lie to each other, lack trust in one another, abuse each other emotionally and sometimes physically, lack effective communication, and chase each other away. There are many couples not happy being together anymore, hence why divorce rates are so high.

There tend to be so many issues and, unfortunately, those issues weigh so heavy on people for so long that they feel the only option is to split up or get a divorce. Issues can be corrected as long as both parties stay open to change. It absolutely can't be one-sided. One-sided doesn't work. Teamwork leads to improvement. Both of you have to be willing to compromise and make changes.

Melinda and I have been together since 2008. People look at where we are now and say things like, "Well of course you guys are happy, look at your life!" Obviously, they don't know the struggle we went through. You do now and know the amount of ups and downs we have battled over the years. But here's the thing: even with everything we struggled with, from the food stamps to living in a dangerous neighborhood and sleeping on a couch, our relationship has pretty much remained the same. Does that mean we haven't had our issues? Of course not. I will address one big issue we had in our marriage in the communication section, but for the most part we have been a very happy couple, don't argue much, trust one another completely, and have an incredible sex life. Sex is an important part of any marriage. But my goal in this part of the book is to help you improve your relationship with your significant other. Do your best to get them to read this section along with you, especially if you both are struggling.

Trust

Trust provides the foundation for any relationship. What the hell happened to trusting one another? It's rare anymore that I come across a couple that truly trusts each other completely. The amount of people I know who check each other's social media accounts or phones daily is off the charts. Happiness in a relationship cannot happen if you don't trust one another. Every couple that I've ever known with trust issues hasn't had a good relationship and normally ends up splitting up.

Now listen, I get it, maybe your spouse cheated at one point and that's why you're creeping her account. However, that doesn't give you a right to invade her privacy. Plus, if you are still together, you forgave her at some point or at least told her that you had. Did you not actually mean it? If you did, then why are you still putting yourself through the mental torment of believing something is still going on? When you forgive someone, you give them another chance until they mess up again. If they mess up again then you consider ending the relationship or seeking professional help. There's nothing wrong with couples therapy.

The amount of stress you experience by constantly checking her social media messages and thinking she might be cheating again harms you and her. It makes it incredibly hard to enjoy each other's company, say on date night, if all you're thinking about is whether she's sitting there and thinking about another guy. And by the way, I'm using "her" in this example so I don't have to keep saying "him and her" the entire time. Guys are just as guilty. How are you ever going to be happy as a couple if all you're thinking about is "oh man I hope she's not cheating on me again"? You can't. It's impossible. You have to trust each other fully.

If you cheated, don't cheat again. It's as simple as that. If you're lucky enough to be forgiven by your spouse, don't make the same mistake again. If you do continue to cheat, you deserve everything coming your way. At the same time, if you truly are a changed person and were completely forgiven, then don't feel it's OK for your spouse to control every part of your life by continuing to be jealous, limit who you talk to, or constantly check your social media accounts. Speak up! Talk to her about it. Tell her that it's not OK. It's not. It's not right that you are being dragged down repeatedly for past mistakes. Stand up for yourself! We all have made mistakes. Good lord, if Melinda constantly judged me for all the mistakes I've made, we would be a mess. I have never cheated on her, of course, but I have made mistakes. We both don't judge each other for our past mistakes. It's important for your relationship that you have the same approach.

I don't worry what Melinda does and she doesn't worry about what I do. It's been that way for a long time. We respect each other enough not to cheat on one another. Do you hear that? Yes, you have to respect your spouse by not giving them a reason not to trust you. If you don't respect your spouse, you're just not a good partner. But I'm talking to women all day long. It's a part of my business. With the amount of women I email, message, work with and mentor, if she didn't trust me it would drive her absolutely crazy! But she does, and it's never been a problem.

I know many people who are constantly held back from pursuing a business opportunity because their spouse is afraid of him or her talking to other people of the same sex. Talking to people is a necessity for business success. That's a fact. If you're this type of person, you really have to think about what you're doing. You mean to tell me you can't allow your spouse to pursue a business opportunity that could positively impact your family's life because of your insecurities? Get over yourself. You're only creating issues within your marriage, whether your spouse talks about it or not. Many people hold things in until they reach that boiling point. Push them far enough, though, and they will explode.

Melinda also knows that one of the worst things anyone can do to me is break my trust and she respects that. With the way I am, if I put trust in someone, I don't half-ass trust them, I fully do so. Once they break that trust, first of all it crushes me, but then normally I end the relationship, just depending on who it's with. If it's someone very close to me, the only way I would trust them again is if we both sat down and discussed the situation like adults and I felt that they were being honest about not breaking that trust again. Normally, I can tell and so can you. Our gut is like our second brain. The phrase "gut feeling" didn't come out of nowhere. Normally, when I have a gut feeling that something's wrong or that someone is trying to screw me over, it's pretty accurate. It's important to listen to it.

When you can trust one another fully, a weight lifts off your shoulders. It's one less thing to worry about. If you currently don't trust your significant other, though, it's time to have a discussion. You can't continue in the relationship if all you can think about is whether or not he or she is talking to someone else. If you just ignore it like most people do, it will fester and shit will hit the fan. It's like putting a Mentos in a bottle of coke and watching it explode and spray everywhere! You don't want that happening. It's best to calmly talk to your partner before it ever gets to that point. Discuss it like adults and work out a solution.

Maybe you had a rough life growing up as a kid. Maybe your parents created so much distrust that it's extremely hard for you to trust anyone. Listen, I get it. It's a hard thing to deal with, absolutely. However, if you married your spouse and he or she is a good person, as hard as it is for you to do, you have to become vulnerable and trust. If you don't, mark my words, it will create problems in your marriage. You married the person because you love them. If you love them, you need to trust them no matter how rough your past has been.

One last thing, if you are going to forgive your spouse for a mistake made in her past, forgive her and move on. Don't keep bringing it up whenever you have an argument. It's not right for you to bring it up just because you're pissed off. It's not fair to her. There's a good chance she already felt bad for the situation, so don't repeatedly make her feel bad for something she did 10 years ago. If I mess up with something with someone and I admit that it was my fault, I apologize and make whatever adjustments I have to. I don't want to be at dinner 10 years down the road and it comes up again. I never want to hear about it again. That's how it should be.

Communication

Trust forms a foundation for a relationship, but so does communication. If you don't communicate with your spouse, it will lead to a number of issues. When something bothers either of you, you have to actually communicate the problem. If not, it just builds up and gets to the point like I mentioned in the last section. That's no good for anyone. You both can't just ignore that there's a problem. An issue doesn't just go away on its own! Every issue has to be addressed in a timely manner.

Melinda and I have great communication now, but it hasn't always been this way. We went through a very rough time back in 2012 because of a lack of communication. I'm going to open up and share something with you that I don't share too often.

We waited to try for our second child until we were financially sound. When she got pregnant again, we were ecstatic! However, when we went in for our check-up, we discovered that the baby had no heartbeat. When we had to have the procedure done to remove the lifeless fetus, it was pretty traumatizing for Melinda. To make matters worse, she had a number of issues during the procedure and it scared me to death. But after we lost the baby, neither of us talked about it. In the past, I always liked to deal with things internally. I've never been the type of person to open up and talk about how I'm feeling. We just went on ignoring that there was an issue. It destroyed her inside so much that she started changing. She became almost depressed. I had no idea there was even a problem because she never talked to me about it. I just believed it was her way of dealing with things too. And then she started opening up with others instead of talking to me.

Without going into too much detail, we had a situation occur months later and it led to a massive fallout between us. It got so bad that I was sure that our marriage wasn't going to last. Instead of calling it quits, though, we decided to sit down and figure out a solution. We both talked about the issues we were having and what we were feeling after the miscarriage. For the first time, we were truly communicating. We made a pact that, from that point forward, we would communicate with each other the moment we felt something amiss. We have been doing that since and it's been incredible for our relationship.

When a problem crops up, it has to be addressed quickly. It can't be something that you both dwell on for weeks or months on end. The quicker you can discuss it, the better. Sometimes, though, one or both of you will be very angry. Being angry is OK, but you can't sit down and communicate the issues through anger. You have to discuss it in a calm manner. When you both are pissed off, all that ends up happening is that you yell at each other. Then someone says something they don't mean and things go south rather quickly.

Once one person attacks the other, the flood gates open and it's just nothing but attacks back and forth. It's like two sharks repeatedly biting chunks out of one another! That can never happen. If you ever get so angry that you feel like you're going to lash out with harmful words, walk away. Tell your spouse that you need some time to cool down because you don't want to say something that will hurt her. When you're furious you can't think straight. When you walk away, have some time alone, take a deep breath and calm yourself down, you can then think about how you're going to approach the situation without getting too upset or upsetting your spouse. Once you're both completely calmed down, you can meet and agree to stay calm.

Many people, especially men, hate to be wrong. Even if we are wrong, most of the time we won't admit it. Instead, we will find some way to turn it around and put blame on our spouse. It's important that, if you're wrong, you admit you're wrong. It takes a strong person to admit fault and apologize! You have to put your stubbornness to the side for the sake of the relationship. There have been many times that I have messed up and will take the blame for it. Melinda is the same way. When we are wrong, we have no issue owning up to it. The problems come when one person blames the other for every issue that's ever arisen in the relationship. That's not a relationship, that's more like a dictatorship. It's a good way to chase your spouse away. There has to be a mutual understanding that it's quite possible that both of you are to blame. Once the person at fault takes proper blame, then you can work together in discovering a solution.

Here is the step-by-step process you can use when an issue occurs in your relationship.

Step 1 - Immediately ask your spouse to sit down and talk about something that's bothering you.

Step 2 - Both of you calm down before addressing the situation.

Step 3 - Once calm, communicate the issue, but don't immediately blame the other. Tell him or her how you are feeling and why you are feeling that way.

Step 4 - Give him or her a chance to respond.

Step 5 - Whoever's fault it was should admit fault and apologize.

Step 6 - You communicate together on what changes, if any, should be made to correct the situation.

Step 7 - Apply those changes immediately.

Step 8 - When he or she apologizes and means it, accept the apology and don't bring up the issue again.

Sometimes, though, one spouse might want to handle the situation properly, but the other won't. Maybe you use the process above, but your spouse blows a gasket every time something happens. If that's the case, there is nothing wrong with seeking professional help. In fact, I encourage it. A therapist will sit you both down and help you figure out a solution.

Date your spouse

Do you date your spouse? No? Why not? Is it because of time? Time is an excuse, remember. Is it money? Same thing. Kids? You guessed it. All excuses. In the beginning of the relationship and sometimes even a few years into it, dating is common. It's an important time for you to communicate, connect, and learn about the person. But for some reason, once most couples get married the date nights stop. And then when they have kids, they forget what a date night even means. People will go years and years without spending any quality time with their spouse. That's awful. And you wonder why so many couples have issues! They don't have an opportunity to reconnect with one another on a regular basis.

It doesn't matter what financial situation Melinda and I have been in, whether or not we've had kids, how busy we've been, it's always been a priority to have a date night at least once a week. We do so because we understand how important it is for our relationship. It gives us an opportunity to communicate. It gives us an opportunity to reconnect after a busy week. It gives us an opportunity to have a break from the kids and enjoy each other's company.

During the week, we are both busy. Not only am I always working hard with my businesses, but Melinda cooks all the food, takes care of the kids, and works her business as well. During the week, there just isn't much "us time." That date night allows us some "us time." It's much-needed and comes at just the right time. In the beginning, when we were on food stamps, we couldn't really afford to go out to a nice restaurant and then to a bar, so we had a "date night in" instead. Once our daughter went to bed, we hung out just like we would do if we went out. We had a late dinner, talked to each other, and maybe watched a movie afterward. Once our businesses became successful, then we were able to hire a sitter and go out.

If you want to be happier, reconnect with your spouse, have better sex, create great memories, then have a date night. If you want to continue arguing and feel totally disconnected from your spouse, then don't. Not too hard of a choice.

Here are some date night rules:

1. **It's non-negotiable.** It's too easy to cancel. You're not allowed to do so. Date night has to be non-negotiable every single week. Your best bet is to do what we do and pick a specific date night. Ours is Tuesday night. Of course, there are the rare exceptions, such as an emergency or traveling, but for the most part you should plan on doing date night on the same night every week.

2. **Shut off or at least silence your phones.** What is the point of going on a date if you both are on your phones the whole time? You might as well have stayed home. I can't tell you how many times we've been at a restaurant and

seen a couple not say a word to each other. Rather, their thumbs are moving as fast as lightning as they're texting their friends or browsing social media. You can disconnect for a few hours. If you can't, you've got a problem. If you have kids, only answer the call if it's from the sitter. Don't answer any other calls and ignore text messages or any social media notifications unless it's an emergency. All of your attention should be on your spouse and only your spouse.

3. **Actually talk to each other.** It's quite hilarious when you see a couple on their first date that have no idea what to say to each other, so they sit there in the most awkward silence you've ever experienced. Believe it or not, though, this happens to married couples as well. Let's say they just started going on date night again after not doing so for five years. There might have been so much disconnect that they might not even really know their spouse anymore. So many people go through their daily routines without as much as saying a word to one another until they lay down for bed! It happens. But ask your spouse how she's doing. Ask her about the good things that are going on in her life right now. Also ask her about the bad things. Ask her about her goals. Ask her how she feels about certain situations. Just have a conversation with her! Once you connect again, it can spice back up the relationship.

4. **Show affection.** Chances are, especially if you have kids, that you haven't shown each other affection in quite some time. Tell your wife she looks beautiful. Hold her hand. Give her a kiss. Ladies, you can do the same thing. Tell your man how hot he looks. Grab his ass. Do what you have to do to make your spouse feel sexy again.

5. **Have fun.** You guys don't have to do the normal dinner and a movie. I'm not saying there is anything wrong with that

because Melinda and I do it all the time. But it's nice to do something different every once in a while. Go bowling, go biking, hike through the woods, get drunk while painting, have a picnic, sing karaoke, go see a play, or go skinny dipping. There are a lot of options. You just have to be creative.

Make time daily for your spouse

Yes, you will have date night every single week, but that's not enough. No matter how busy you may be, you have to schedule time with your spouse every night. As a business owner and entrepreneur, I'm about as busy as it comes, but come 8 p.m., I leave my phone in the other room and spend some time with Melinda. We don't do anything crazy, but we might sit right next to each other and watch our favorite shows together. This should be another non-negotiable. It's too easy to let a business call come in and let it interfere with that time with your spouse. You can't allow that to happen.

Take care of your health

I've focused a lot of attention on health in this book. I'm going to focus on it briefly again because it's very important in this section. When you are healthy, you feel good. When you're unhealthy, you don't feel good. That's obvious. But health issues that are controllable and preventable can lead to a lot of issues in a marriage. For example, if you are very obese, there's a good chance you have a number of issues that go along with that. I'm using obesity as an example because 98% of the time, it is preventable and can be reversed with the proper changes to nutrition and adding in exercise.

Anyway, when you face health issues, it's not an enjoyable process. You're down, sometimes depressed, can be quite negative, and all that affects your spouse because you are around her constantly. Negativity spreads like wildfire, especially to those who you're around the most. It can be as much mentally and physically draining on her as it is on you. I don't think this is fair for anyone to have to go through. I could never put Melinda through that.

When I was going through Lyme, one of the toughest things I had to deal with was making sure this didn't happen. Of course, this was a little different situation because Lyme really wasn't preventable, but nonetheless I didn't want her to be affected by my illness. I tried to be as positive as I could. I didn't want her knowing how much pain I was in. I didn't want her to know how bad I struggled mentally. Yes, I talked about it with her some because I needed someone to talk to, but at the same time I didn't want to bring her down with me. Part of my reason for getting healthy again was so that I could be the husband I wanted and needed to be for her.

And by the way, she was incredibly supportive throughout that entire journey. That's just how she is, though. She worried about me so much, which put a lot of stress on her. I hated that. I didn't want her to be stressed out because of something I was dealing with. But when you don't take care of yourself, health issues will arise. That's inevitable. When you do take care of yourself, though, you'll have fewer health issues and therefore the happier you'll be. When you're happy, your spouse is happy.

When you're fit, you look and feel good and are more confident in yourself. All of those matter a lot for your relationship. Part of the reason I take care of myself daily is because I want to look good for my wife. I want her to look at me and be like "holy shit, take off your clothes!" I want her to find me sexy and attractive! I personally feel that looking good for your spouse is an important part of a relationship. Be healthy for you. Be healthy for confidence. Be healthy to look good naked. Be healthy for your sex life. Be healthy to be happy. All of that will be beneficial to your relationship with your spouse.

Provide support

I already covered this earlier in the book, but it's so important for you to support your spouse when she tries to better herself or the family. For example, it makes no sense that there are so many people who discourage their spouse from starting a side business that could potentially lead to financial security. If it's a legit opportunity with excellent potential, there is absolutely no reason not to offer support! Unfortunately, I see it all the time with the type of business that I'm in. Some people even have to hide it from their spouse! Support your spouse. If not, you're going to chase him or her away. Encourage her along the way as well. You don't know how much it will mean for her when you tell her how proud you are of her and that she's doing an incredible job.

Tips for better sex

Ah yeah, I'm about to get all steamy up in here! Just had a flash-back to a DMX song. Awesome. #Nostalgia. But we all love sex. Well maybe not all of us, but the majority of us. I know there are some weird-ass conditions where sex is painful. If you're dealing with that, I feel sorry for you, truly, because sex is amazing. Let me ask you this. How many married couples do you know that don't have sex? Or if they do have sex, maybe it's once every quarter? It seems that it's become generally accepted that the longer you've been married the less sex you're going to have until it disappears all together. That's depressing.

I've had conversations with couples my age who will mention that the last time they had sex was on their anniversary 8 months ago. 8....months. Just think about that for a second. That couple gets it in maybe twice a year. When people say this to Melinda and me, we kind of look at each other like "Oh good lord, I feel bad for them." Then once we aren't around them, we talk about it like two crazy high school girls gossiping. When you're 10 years into being together, you should be having sex at least a couple times a week. Melinda and I have a great sex life. We don't have a problem talking about it. It's a part of every marriage (or at least should be).

So, here's what I'm going to do. I'm going to give you some incredible tips on how to have a better sex life with your significant other.

1. **Stop being so damn boring!** You wonder why your sex life is stagnant, but you only do missionary position right before you head to bed. It becomes a chore. It should not be a chore! It should be fun. It should be spontaneous. Nobody wants sex to be scheduled. And seriously, if you're someone who schedules sex, you've got some issues. Rather, try this. Move around your house and do it at different times. In the middle of the day one day, grab your spouse and head to the nearest closet. What about on top of the washing machine? If you've got a patio, become a rebel and do it in your chair swing. Got a hot tub? That could be fun. Living room couch anyone? The options are endless! Break out of your routine and try something different.

2. **Go on date night once a week.** Yes, date night is important for communication, but it's great for your sex life as well. When you can reconnect, it gets the juices flowing a little bit. You can even tease some while you're out on the date. Fellas, maybe slide your hand up her leg at dinner. Ladies, there are options for you as well. You can kiss him and then nibble a little on his ear. Just a little bit of teasing

can lead to you both wanting to rip the clothes off of each other the moment you walk in the door! Or just not even make it into the house. The car can be fun. If you drive an SUV, the back seats normally come down. Plenty of room. Even if the seats don't come down, there are a ton of options as well. Reverse cowgirl in the front seat, just saying.

3. **Use toys.** Sex toys are great! Let me pause. I'm seriously wondering just how many of you are reading this with your mouths wide open like "damn, did he really just say that?" Yes, yes I did. I warned you all in the beginning, no filter! It's just a straightforward approach to helping you experience success in many aspects of life, including sex. But anyways, sex toys are for adults of all ages. They can be fun. Don't be afraid to bust them out every once in a while, maybe after date night. Oh, and by the way, you can always go to a sex store on date night to pick them out. That's one great way to get you both excited for what's to come afterwards!

4. **Get away.** If your sex life is stagnant, a weekend getaway might be just what you need to spice it back up. This has to be without the kids, of course. Get grandma and grandpa to watch the kids for the weekend and go camping. Camping out in the middle of nowhere is a great place for you guys to have some fun and be as loud as you want! If you don't like the outdoors, that sucks, but a hotel would be fine as well. When you're away from the normal stresses of life, you tend to relax and want to have more sex.

5. **Spoil your spouse.** Hey boys, when was the last time you got your lady flowers? Anniversaries and holidays don't count. I'm talking about randomly showing up after work one day with a big bouquet of flowers in your hand. If you don't, you need to start. Or you can just do something that

you don't normally do, like help clean up the house, do the dishes, or cook dinner one night. Maybe one night tell her that you'll stay at home with the kids while she goes out and gets her nails or hair done. Go out of your way to do something special for her! And ladies, the same goes with you. Maybe organize a day that your husband can go to the bar with all his buddies and watch some football. Both men and women have stressful lives. We get so caught up in our routine that we forget to make our spouse feel special. Once you do, though, it shows them you care. That can reignite the fire.

6. **Stop worrying.** There is nothing that kills the mood more than stress. If you both are stressed out, the last thing you will want to do is get on top of each other. That means you have to find different ways to reduce stress. Massages are great. Take 30 minutes to disconnect from all electronics and turn on some relaxing music. Yoga is good, too. If you have to meditate, then meditate. There are a lot of options.

Have separate guy and girl time

It's great to spend time with one another, but it's important that you allow "guy" and "girl" time as well. This is when you mind the household and your spouse can go out and spend time with friends. This is another one of those things that can't be lopsided. Unfortunately, it is for a lot of couples. One parent will be working and watching the kids the entire time while the other does whatever he or she wants with friends. It can't be this way. It's not fair. You both have to be in agreement that there will be times, whether that's once a week, every two weeks, or every month, that you have a designated "guys day" or "girls day." You need that as a couple. Women need to connect with each other. Guys need to be just guys with one another and do stupid shit. Melinda and I have a great understanding that we each need that time with our friends. Maybe you watch the kids when she goes out and vice versa. But make it a priority. You don't want to be that couple that has no friends! Plus, a great way for you to chase friends away is by constantly telling them "no" when they ask you to do something with them.

HOW TO BE A GOOD PARENT

I fear for our children and future generations because of the direction we are going. It's sad. Childhood obesity is at an all-time high. Kids throw fits when they don't get what they want. Parents always give in. Kids can't trust their parents to follow through with their word. Parents lie to kids and kids lie to parents. Integrity is lost. Values are lost. Children expect things to be handed to them without having to work for it. Bullying has gotten worse. There is as much disconnect between parents and their kids as between the parents themselves because of electronics. It's a tough time to be a parent! All of us parents have to understand, though, that we have the ability to influence and mold our children.

This is going to be a section that you may not particular like, not because what I'm about to share isn't correct, but rather because it's going to hit home and make you realize that you've been making a lot of mistakes with how you're raising your kids. And you know what? That's OK. I still make mistakes as a father. Melinda still makes mistakes as a mother. We aren't perfect. The key is that we keep adjusting and getting better as parents. The problem comes when we realize issues exist but don't take any steps to correct them. It's time for you to take necessary action to make sure your kids are on the right path to happiness, good health, and success.

Leading by example

Like it or not, as parents we are leaders by example. We set the example for our children to follow. You've got to understand that every day those little eyes watch you, study you, mimic you. You are what they will become. How's that feel? If you look in the mirror today, would you be happy if your children become who you are? If you really think about it, it's a tough thing to swallow, isn't it? Or maybe it's not. Maybe you are being that good example that you need to be.

You have to remember that you set the example with every aspect of your life, such as how you treat others, your health, your relationships, your integrity, your work ethic and so on and so forth. Every decision you make, whether it's a big or small one, has some sort of effect not just on you, but your children as well. Once you're well aware of the type of impact your actions can have on your children, you tend to make much better decisions. Being conscious of your choices helps you create a better life for yourself and raise your kids the right way.

Next, I'm going to go into detail about how to lead by example in three important areas: being healthy, treating your spouse properly, and living with integrity.

Being healthy

Most parents purposely play ignorant to the fact that their health choices affect their children. Once again, it's easier to remain inside that comfort zone and ignore reality than to take action and make a change. But here's reality: Making poor health choices leads to potentially developing obesity, disease, or even cancer. That's not made up. That's a fact. Burying the truth deep in your mind that you are or will be the reason why your kid suffers from all these problems is much easier than being fully conscious about it and experiencing the pain that will be associated with that realization.

And trust me, once you stop ignoring it, it will be painful. You will look at your kids and realize that you are leading them down a path of destruction. Maybe they are obese, maybe already dealing with many illnesses. That pain might feel like a punch in the gut, but it will be a move in the right direction because you will never want to experience that feeling again. Pain like that causes a shift. There is nothing worse as a parent than the feeling of failing your children. Trust me, I've been there. I pray that you don't ever have to experience that yourself, but sometimes that's what it will take for you to change course.

Why do most people ignore the truth when it comes to this? A lot of it has to do with instant gratification. They focus so much on things directly in front of them, rather than on how each decision they make affects their children's future. For example, when they order a large pizza for the family, they only care about how good it's going to taste. They don't care about how eating pizza on a consistent basis can cause weight gain and a suppressed immune system from all the sugar and unhealthy fat.

Another reason for ignoring the truth is the fact that they have to make a change in their lifestyle. As I talked about in the "Changing Your Mindset" section, change can be scary. So many people fear change because they don't know what's ahead. "So, you're telling me I will have to get rid of all the foods I enjoy?" "I will have to put effort into working out daily?" "I will be so sore that I won't be able to move?" That fear of change is strong enough to cause them to bury the truth and continue with their poor choices. But it shouldn't be. Your children should trump all your fear.

Think about it this way. Let's say you don't know how to swim and are afraid of water because of a past experience. One day your two-year-old accidentally gets outside and falls into the deep end of your pool. You run outside and see her about to go under. I'd say 100% of the time you are going to jump in and save her! That fear will be put to the side for the safety of your child! Your fear of change should be put aside for the health of your children as well.

Our children don't have a choice. I believe this is the part that pisses me off the most. It kills me inside when I see an 8-year-old who weighs almost as much as I do. Then you see the parents who are both 400 lbs. each. Do you mean to tell me that it's not the parent's fault that their kid is obese? Come on. Stop with that bullshit. It's absolutely the parent's fault! They can deny it all they want, but it is their fault. Eventually they will have to take ownership.

When kids are young, they don't know better. They just follow our lead. If we are eating right, they will eat right. And remember, we make the choices for them. They will eat what we put in front of them. If we are exercising daily, there's a good chance they will do the same when they grow up. I can't tell you how many times I walk in and see both of my girls working out with Melinda. She does it for them just as I do it for them. My children are my "why." I don't need motivation to eat right or work out consistently because I know the positive impact I have on them by doing so.

If you're a parent who hasn't led by example up until this point, what can you do? The great thing is that you can always change. It's never too late to change course. First, make a change in your own life. If you're not taking care of yourself, it's time to start. Get yourself on a workout and nutrition plan. Make sure your kids eat the same foods you eat. Will they be happy about it? No. Does it matter? It shouldn't. Again, they don't know better. All they know at this point is being loaded with sugar and enjoying the feeling and taste that comes with it. They don't know how excess sugar consumption affects their health, but you do.

With my kids, they either eat what we feed them or they don't eat. It's as simple as that. We also do our best to explain to them why we have them eat healthier. The older they get, the more they understand. And the great thing, too, is that there are a ton of healthier options for some of their favorite foods, such as pizza, chicken fingers, fries, etc. "Healthy" doesn't have to be gross. You might discover that they actually prefer the healthier versions! But your kids' health starts with you. Start making better decisions daily for both you and them.

Treating spouse properly

I've witnessed parents scream at each other in front of their children. Sometimes it gets so bad that it looks like it's going to get physical. The crazy part about it all that it's in public! If it's that bad in public, imagine how bad it is in private. Once again, those little eyes are always watching. If you treat your spouse with disrespect, you're teaching them to eventually do the same in their relationships. The old saying "the apple doesn't fall too far from the tree" is true. It's common that you see a son whose father abused his mother grow up to abuse his spouse as well.

But on the flip side, if a son grows up watching his father respect his mother, there's a great chance he more than likely will respect his future wife. If you handle an argument with your spouse like I talked about in the "Communication" section, you're teaching your children how to treat others properly. My parents were this way. Sure, they argued from time to time, but in the end, they both respected each other, and the argument eventually got handled properly. My sister and I saw that. It's why we both have so much respect for our spouses. My parents led by example. Treat your spouse right if you want your kids to eventually do the same.

Living with & teaching integrity

The best way to teach your kids integrity is to live your life with integrity. They will adopt the morals and values you use every single day. Lack integrity, though, and they will do the same. Are you honest with others? Can others trust you? Do you always do the right thing in tough situations? These questions you must ask yourself. My parents talked to me quite often about honesty and doing the right thing, but I learned mostly by how they acted. They always operated with integrity with everything they did. If you want your children to have integrity, you must do the same.

Let your kids fail

Why have we have been trying so hard to keep our kids from failing? It's evident everywhere we look, especially in sports. Kids are praised for losing. Everything is wrong with that. When I was a kid and we lost a baseball tournament, I didn't get a trophy for losing. Rather, our coach made us work twice as hard at practice on all the things we messed up with during the games. Nobody enjoyed losing.

Now those who lose seem content with it. If everyone "wins," how is anyone ever going to learn the importance of failing and adjusting? Failure is a necessity for success, remember? If failure evaporates from a child's life, we fail to teach them one of the most important life lessons they need to learn at a young age. As you already know, you have to fail to move forward. We accomplish nothing without experiencing some sort of failure and then adjusting and putting in the effort to change.

My middle child, Alaina, hates to lose. I mean she hates it with a passion. That's good. I don't want her to enjoy losing. However, most parents let their children win, such as with a game, to avoid having them lose and feel upset about it. When they reach a certain age and can comprehend what you're talking about, it's important that you don't let this happen. Whenever we play a game and Alaina loses, I tell her that losing is OK. It's OK because we learn from it and make changes so that we get better. When all of my kids are old enough to play competitive sports, if they get a participation trophy, they are going to understand that the trophy means nothing and that they need to work hard so that they do eventually win the trophies that count.

Allow your children to fail. The more they fail, the more they learn. At the same time, though, make sure they understand how to handle failure. If they don't understand it, they won't learn from it properly. Once they understand the failure process, as I explained earlier in the book, then they can really begin to move toward having success with everything that they do.

Designated kid time

I talked about the importance of setting aside time for your spouse each evening and having a date night once a week. You need to do the same with your kids. The same rules apply. No technology (unless it's an activity with your kid), no work, and all of your attention needs to be on them. Each night I stop working at 5 p.m., put my phone in another room on silent, and spend an hour or two with my kids. Normally I play hide-and-seek, tag, or soccer with my girls and then spend about an hour chasing my boy around or watching car videos with him. The little dude (he's two years old at the time of writing this) is obsessed with cars just like his daddy. I hop on Instagram and bring up sports car videos and he lays in my lap and watches them nonstop! It's just something we enjoy doing together.

That quality time means the world to them. It meant the world to me growing up. My parents would get home after work and play some sort of game with my sister and I or take us fishing down at our pond. Even as we got older, that one-on-one time meant the world to me.

Just like a date night with your spouse, you need to do something similar with your kids each week. If you have more than one kid like I do, you can either take them all out or do something with them individually. If my daughters want to do something separately, then I might spend a few hours with one, bring her back home and then take the other one out for a few hours. What can you do? There are so many options. You can take them out to dinner, go golfing, go fishing, go hiking, or even take them painting. As they get older, you can then begin taking them on trips. I can't wait until my kids are old enough to start doing some of the outdoor activities with me that I'm passionate about, such as snowboarding, camping, and dirt bike riding. I want them to enjoy taking trips with me. I want to be their best friend. I will be a parent when I need to be a parent, of course, but I want a relationship with them like I have with my best friends.

One of my good friends does something with his kids that I will do once mine are old enough. I absolutely love this idea. He takes each of his kids on a trip with just him. His wife does the same. It allows them to spend one-on-one quality time together. Of course, this requires money and time to happen. Even more reason to start up a side business!

My kids will always come first. No matter how many businesses I'm running, how much I'm traveling to speak, they will be the number one priority in my life. My businesses will never come before them! I will make sure of it. Unfortunately, though, there's too many people where this isn't the case. Their priorities are messed up and work comes before spending time with their kids. I believe that one of the worst regrets anyone can have on their deathbed is that they didn't spend enough time with their kids. When your boy asks you to do something with him, do it. If you have the opportunity to travel with your son and create incredible memories, take it. If you don't and consistently put work before your kids, you will push them away. Then eventually you will be too old to do those things. You never want that to happen. You want to stay close to them and keep that relationship strong! One day when I'm old, I'm going to look back at all the incredible memories I created with my children and be completely satisfied.

Make your kids a priority. Spend time with them every day. Take them out to do something once a week. Take them on trips they will remember for a lifetime! Just remember, there will always be work to do. Take that break, take that vacation, and spend quality time with them whenever you have the opportunity to do so.

Following through on your word

I've watched a lot of movies where the boy has an event like a karate match and looks out to the crowd looking for his father who promised he would be there. He sees the seat next to his mom open and knows that dad isn't going to make it yet again. You see his smile turn to a frown and he gets sad. It then cuts to a scene where the father is still at work and keeps getting caught up with calls and other work-related activities. He keeps looking at his watch, knowing damn well he's cutting it close. He gets his work done, hits a ton of traffic, and by the time he arrives to the event, it's over.

When you tell your children that you're going to do something, you better make sure you do it. No, not 50% of the time, all the time. When you don't follow through with your word, whether you believe so or not, it has a pretty big effect on them emotionally. It really brings them down. When I played baseball as a kid, my parents came to just about every single game. When they told me they would be there, they were there, no questions about it. It established trust between us. I'm the same way with my kids. If I tell them that I'm going to take them to the park on Thursday, I make sure I take them to the park on Thursday. If I tell them I'm going to go for a bike ride with them, I go on a bike ride with them. If I promise my kids that I would do something, no matter what comes up, I do it. If you want to build trust and a great relationship with your kids, it's important that you do the same.

Establishing trust

Trust is everything. If we catch any of our kids lying to us, there are major consequences. I believe it's one of the worst things that you can do to the people you care about most. When we were growing up, my parents really stressed the importance of honesty, no matter what the situation may be. They communicated with us, we communicated with them. Our kids have learned the same thing. I want them to be honest with Melinda and I about everything. We will do the same with them. It's important that you establish trust within your relationship with your children as well. Talk to them about it.

Teaching work ethic

My kids know that if they want something, they have to work for it. We don't just give them toys because they want toys. We have them do chores around the house and for each chore they get a point. For every 10 points they get $5. If one of my girls wants a

$40 doll, for example, she knows that she has to do 80 chores. If we are out shopping and one of them asks for a toy, but doesn't have the points, we tell them "no."

I think that "no" is a word that isn't used enough with parents. Many times, a child will ask for something and the parents will just get it for them. That's teaching them entitlement. Then they grow up to be adults and expect everything to be handed to them. Rather, teach them young that, if they want something, they are going to have to put in effort to get it. When my children get their first car, they will have to make payments on it. When they go to college, we are going to make them pay for it, or at least part of it all depending if we decide to reward them for graduating high school with honors. That's preparing them for the real world.

My parents made me pay for part of my college and I'm glad they did because I had to work hard to pay off my student loans. It taught me responsibility. When my children become adults, I want them understanding that, if they want to be successful in business, with their relationships, and with their health, they are going to have to work for it. As you've learned from this book, that's the only way to find success anyway. Teach your kids to be the hardest workers they know.

Talking about the hard stuff

There are some major things that every parent has to eventually discuss with their children. Bullying is one. Bullying is very serious and can really tear down children emotionally. I know because I've been through it. It was one of the hardest things I ever had to go through. But I never really talked about it with my parents. I kept it inside. They never knew there was an issue.

We constantly communicate with our kids about bullying, treating others right, and what to do if they're being bullied. I ask Madison, our oldest, all the time if anyone picks on her at school because if so, then Melinda and I can address it with her, the school, and possibly the parents of the bully. It's crucial that she knows that she can talk to us about anything, especially bullying. If you don't talk about bullying with your children and they end up being bullied, it can lead to some serious consequences. You want to prevent that from happening.

Drugs and alcohol is another. I went to a Catholic High School and you would think that drugs wouldn't be an issue there, but they were. Students commonly sold drugs in the parking lot after school. I always refused because my parents talked to me about the importance of staying away from drugs and the addictions and other issues associated with them. This is something they discussed with my sister and me at a very young age.

They also talked about staying away from alcohol. Kids binge-drink, which can be incredibly dangerous and cause them to be in situations they don't want to be in. I didn't have my first sip of alcohol until I graduated high school. Even when I did start drinking, though, I was never irresponsible. I had some good times, especially through college, but I never drank to the point where I couldn't comprehend what was happening around me. My parents taught me to be very responsible when drinking. I will talk to my kids about these issues as well when they are old enough to understand. You should do the same.

You've got to talk about sex. At the time of writing this book, I've been fortunate enough to not have to do this yet, but I know it's coming eventually. My parents didn't talk about it too much, but they did explain the repercussions of unprotected sex. It wasn't all about getting an STD or getting a girl pregnant at a young age.

There have been shows on television that feature girls getting pregnant at 15 or 16 years old. Hell no. My kids will be well aware of how their decisions regarding sex can affect their future.

Personal development at a young age

When my kids get to the age where they can read well, they stop getting paid for chores. They still have to do the chores, of course, but that just becomes a part of living in the house. Rather, we pay them $10-$20 (depending on size) for every personal development book they read. They can't lie about reading it, either, because they have to share with us exactly what they learned and how they are going to apply what they learned to their life. We got this idea from John Maxwell. You might want to take a similar approach with your kids. Imagine how much knowledge they will have if they read a hundred personal development books by the time they are 15!

Limiting electronic time

If children had the opportunity, I'm sure they would be on their phones or iPad or playing video games all day long. Maybe that's how your kid is now. It wouldn't surprise me. Kids are glued to their electronics! It's puts them in zombie mode. We can't have zombie mode. Now listen, I have nothing against these things. I think they can be beneficial in a lot of ways. For one, video games give me an opportunity to relax and connect with my friends who are all over the damn country. I don't play often, but I will when my friends are on after I have crossed off everything from my priority list for the day. Kids use video games to connect with their friends. Second, there are many informational learning tools all over the internet. We have programs for our kids that they can watch on their iPads and learn some incredible things.

However, too much electronic time isn't a good thing. Video games, for example, can be addicting. I can see how some kids can spend literally an entire day playing. It also keeps kids sitting still for long periods of time. It's important that your kids are active. When I was younger, my parents made me go outside. Video games were around back then, but they limited how much I could play and forced me to go do something outside. Normally I hiked, went mountain biking, dirt bike riding, or played baseball or kickball in the yard with the neighbors.

It's important that you force your kids to be active as well. In addition, even though they are socializing, they aren't truly socializing. I've come across many kids who are clueless about how to talk to someone face-to-face. There develops a really, really awkward moment when you ask a kid something and he has no idea how to actually respond so he just walks away or doesn't say anything at all. Make sure your kids know how to socialize outside of electronics so that they can actually function in the real world.

What do Melinda and I do? We have a time limit for how long they can be on their electronics daily. That time is an hour a day. We purchased little timers that they press anytime they are using the electronics to start the clock and then, once they are done, they press it again to stop it. Once they get to an hour, they can no longer be on electronics for the rest of the day. In addition, we have a "no electronics during bedtime" rule. When it's time to go to sleep, they need to go to sleep, not hop on their iPads and play games. They have to leave their electronics downstairs with us every night.

Disciplining your children

There have been many times that someone has come up to us while we were out to dinner with the kids and tell us how well-behaved they are. They are well-behaved because they don't have a choice. They know that if they aren't, there will be consequences. Melinda and I have always been very strict with the kids. We have to be! If not, they will walk all over us. I will never have a child who will throw a fit at the checkout line because I won't buy a chocolate bar he wanted. If that ever began to happen with our kids, all I would have to do is give "the look" and they would straighten right up. That's how my parents were with my sister and I, that's how we are with our kids.

Part of the reason our kids are so well-behaved is that Melinda and I always follow through with our threats. For example, if Alaina is acting up, we will tell her that if she doesn't act right we will take her iPad away. If she acts up again, her iPad is taken away. If she continues to act up, it's taken away for multiple days. That's had to happen many times in order for her to understand that if she misbehaves there will be consequences. We have done this with every kid, whether it's by taking away something they enjoy playing with or making them stand in the corner.

When I got in trouble as a kid, my parents made me stand in the corner with my nose literally touching the wall. I wasn't allowed to move or say anything until my parents said that corner time was up. I hated it, but it taught me to act right if I wanted to stay out of the corner. We have done the same with our kids. They don't like it. They're not supposed to like it. We are disciplining them for doing something wrong. By following through with our threats, though, they know that if they don't behave there will be consequences. We give one warning and that's it.

Most parents don't follow through with their threats. They will tell their kid that if he does something again he will get in trouble, but when he does it again they just give more threats. Once the kid knows that you aren't going to follow through, they will continue to misbehave. Then eventually they learn that if they want something, all they have to do is keep throwing a fit until you eventually give in. That's how you end up having a kid that throws fits in the grocery store when he wants that candy bar. That's how you end up with an adult that throws a fit when he doesn't land a job.

From this point on, you can't give empty threats. If your child acts up, discipline him. I think fear of being the "bad guy" holds a lot of parents back. They don't want their kids upset with them. Too many people try to be friends instead of parents. There's a time to be a friend and a time to be a parent. Melinda lets me do most of the disciplining, but she won't hesitate to discipline if one of the kids get out of hand while I'm not around. It's our responsibility as parents to make sure our children listen well, respect others, and act right.

Teaching them to give back

One of the toughest things that Melinda and I constantly deal with and worry about as successful parents is making sure our kids don't ever have a sense of entitlement. Melinda and I both know what it's like to struggle, and even though that struggle was tough to go through, it's a big reason why we are where we are today. Going through those tough times forced us to fight our way out of it. We fought long and hard for years! My kids probably won't ever have to deal with that. So, it becomes a challenge to figure out how we can make sure they grow up understanding just how blessed they are to be in their situation and to teach them the type of grind it takes to achieve success.

One way to do this is by sharing our story with them and helping them understand what all we had to go through to get where we are today. But another way is by opening their eyes to other children who don't have it anywhere remotely close to as good as they do. This was one of the reasons we began adopting less fortunate families for Christmas and lavishing them with gifts. We talked to our kids about why we were doing it (because it's good to help those who need help) and even had them pick out the toys for the children. It was such a neat experience watching them get excited because they knew they were helping someone else. It was a proud moment as a parent! After they picked out the toys, if it was safe, we would take them with us to the house to deliver the gifts. Not only did they get to see the very poor living conditions that these kids endured, they also saw how they don't have anything. They then watched the children open the gifts and got to witness the sheer joy when they realized they got what they wanted. I believe at that moment they "got it."

We constantly talk to them about how giving back and helping others is such an important part of life. It leads to real fulfillment. Something else we do is have them go through their toys each year and donate the ones they don't play with anymore. We talk to them about how there are many kids that don't have any toys at all and that any toy that they can give them will make their day. Every single time they end up with bags full of toys.

Are you teaching your kids the importance of giving back and helping others? You might be telling them, but are you showing them? Are you taking them to experience what it feels like to help someone in need? If you don't, you need to. There is no greater feeling than knowing that you're impacting someone's life in a positive way. I want my kids to feel the same way.

How to Be a Good Friend

A lot of the same rules of being a good spouse apply to being a good friend. Not all of them, of course. Some of those rules might get a little weird. But it's all the same when it comes to communication, honesty, prioritizing and support. This section won't be long. I've kept you long enough. Your brain is probably fried. We are close to the end, don't you worry. However, I'm hoping that there was so much information and value jam-packed into the book that it kept your interest the entire way. I've tried to keep it interesting. If I haven't, well I guess that sucks. But what can I do? OK, time for some great tips to wrap this all up.

Stay in contact

While going through school, we have our best friends who we never separate from. You know what I'm talking about. It's those buddies you call up to go bike riding. The ones you constantly get in trouble with. The ones who will back you up if someone starts shit with you. You do everything and would do everything for these boys!

Women, I'm sure it was just a tad different for you. Make-up parties, sleepovers, pillow fights, hell I don't know, I'm just reaching for straws here. To be honest, I have no idea what you girls used to do with each other. But regardless, we all had those people we could rely on that we constantly had a blast with. Come senior year in high school, we all made a pact that we would always stay in contact after school ended. Son of a bitch that was short-lived. The majority of my best friends from school I don't even talk to anymore. It's not that I don't want to because I have tried multiple times to get together and do something, but life just gets in the way. Or is that an excuse? If you ask me, I think so.

I've got a few best friends from school who I still stay in contact with on a regular basis. Throughout the years, even though all of our lives have changed so drastically, and we have become busy with family and work, we still find time to talk and hang out, no matter how far away we are from each other. I grew up in Ohio and live in Texas now, but I still go back home and spend time with my boys and they come visit me as well. That's how it works. You each need to give and take some in order to sustain a friendship. When your friends ask you to get together for a weekend, go do it. If you ask them to get together for a weekend, they need to do the same. Take family trips with one another. Maybe go camping or skiing. Head to the beach for a nice tropical vacation and get drunk and talk about all the good times you had!

Be there for support

You find out who your real friends are when you go through real rough times. The fake ones abandon you, while your true friends call you up every so often to check on you. When I was battling Lyme disease, quite a few friends texted me or called me to ask if I needed to talk. I did need to talk. Lyme was the toughest thing I've ever had to face in my entire life. My friends know I don't like to complain and that I like to keep whatever I'm going through to myself, but they also know that it's not good to do so. They would dig and dig until I opened up to them and talked about my struggles. It was such a relief to be able to do so. They encouraged me and helped me get through it.

Do you support your friends when they are struggling? Do you call them up randomly just to check on them and make sure everything is good? If not, you need to. That's what good friends do. If one of your friends is going through a rough time, whether it's with their family, finances, or career, make sure you are there to support them every step of the way.

Be trustworthy & honest

I've hit on trust and honesty hard throughout this entire book. It basically comes down to this. If you want to keep your friends, be trustworthy and honest with them. If you don't want any friends, then lie and break their trust. It's as easy as that. There's not a quicker way to chase away someone you care about than lying to them or sharing something that they told you in confidence.

Don't gossip about others

Surprisingly, a lot of "friends" will gossip about you behind your back. That's not a true friend. When that happens, it normally gets back to you. I learned a long time ago not to talk about others behind their backs. I made mistakes, formed judgments (usually false ones), talked smack and chased people away. Even when we have friends talking about other friends, I try to keep quiet. I will only talk about what I have no issues saying right to someone's face. My friends know I have no problems saying how I feel. Don't gossip. Not only does it make you look bad, but you can easily hurt people that mean a lot to you.

Make time for your friends

Every week Melinda and I have a date night, but we also have a designated "friends night." We've been doing this for years! Most people have never thought of this before, but we value our friendships so much that we make sure we use one night out of the week to spend time with our friends. We do this together as a couple. If they have kids, sometimes they get sitters and sometimes they don't. Sometimes we all go out to dinner and the bars and have a good time and other times we just relax at someone's house. I think it's important to have a friends night every week because your friends are an important part of your life.

In addition, you all have to unplug from electronics and actually communicate. There is nothing more annoying than talking to someone who is sitting there browsing Instagram, not even listening to a damn word you say. Even though my entire business is online, I still do my best to unplug as much as possible when I'm spending time with friends. Talk to your friends about doing the same. One idea that we have implemented quite a few times while having friends over is to put a basket at the door entrance and everyone who comes in has to put their phones in the basket. They aren't allowed to pick up their phones unless they have to check on their kids or they are leaving. Might want to try that out as well.

CONCLUSION

How's that for a wild ride? Hopefully I was able to live up to your expectations. I covered a lot. The book ended up much longer than I thought it would be, but I also didn't want to skimp on any information. Hopefully somehow, some way, I brought value to your life. That ultimately was my goal.

If you did find it helpful, nothing would be more fulfilling than to get a message or email from you letting me know that this book has changed your life. Seriously, please do it. I will do my best to respond quickly. But I set it all out there for you, got vulnerable a few times, and was as transparent as I could possibly be because I wanted to relate to you and inspire you to change. You now know parts of my story that some of my friends don't even know about!

I've been through an interesting life to this point, learned a lot of lessons, and gained so much wisdom from my past experiences, personal development, and obstacles that I've faced and overcome. Use what I shared as a tool to leverage change in your life. But again, I can't do it for you. Now you are faced with the toughest part of it all. Now you have to actually step outside that comfort zone and take action on what you learned.

Taking action is the key to success. Don't procrastinate. At this very moment, start planning for your future. If you aren't happy with where you currently are with your mindset, health, finances, or relationships, now is the time to change.

If you have any questions for me, I'm going to put all of my contact info below. Don't hesitate to reach out to me. If you would like me to come speak at your event, email me. Follow Melinda and I on Instagram and Facebook. And please leave a positive review for this book if you found it helpful!

Take action. Grind Daily. Eliminate excuses. Conquer your fears. Focus on improving your health. Be a better spouse, parent, and friend. Boom, that's it. Until next time, my friends.

Josh's Instagram: Instagram.com/TheJoshSpencer

Josh's Facebook: Facebook.com/TheJoshSpencer

Josh's Email: Josh@JoshSpencer.com

Melinda's Instagram: Instagram.com/CoachMelinda8

Melinda's Facebook: Facebook.com/MelindaFitness

About the Author

Josh Spencer is a straight-forward, no BS, online fitness coach and network marketing guru that has been able to create a seven-figure business from scratch. He also has battled and conquered a debilitating disease using mostly natural therapies. He has a passion for learning and sharing what he has learned with others so that they, too, can achieve success, especially in the areas of mindset, health, finances, and relationships.

To learn more, or to contact Josh, visit www.Joshspencer.com

Made in the USA
Middletown, DE
22 December 2020